To

_____

From

_____

Message

_____
_____
_____

God's Daily Answers

© 2018 Christian Art Publishers, RSA
   Christian Art Gifts Inc., IL, USA

First edition 2018

Designed by Christian Art Publishers

Images used under license from Shutterstock.com

Copyright © 2017 Meadow's Edge Group, LLC

Content Development by Meadow's Edge Group, LLC

Printed in China

ISBN 978-1-4321-1535-7

19 20 21 22 23 24 25 26 27 28 – 11 10 9 8 7 6 5 4 3 2

God's
DAILY
ANSWERS

Godly Wisdom to
Direct Your Steps

CHRISTIAN ART
PUBLISHERS

There is an appointed
time for everything.
And there is a time for
every event under heaven.

Ecclesiastes 3:1

Introduction

God has given each person the gift of a free and sovereign will. In other words, we have the right to choose for ourselves the path we will take in life. And yet, because He loves us, He stands with hands outstretched, softly urging, "Choose Me, follow Me." His promise is that when we do, He will gently lead us through the maze of available options to the ones that will bring us love, joy, peace and fulfillment.

God's Daily Answers will encourage you to look to Him, your Creator, the one who has always loved you, as you face those crucial choices in life. Take His hand, listen for His voice, read His Word, share the longings of your heart with Him in prayer. God is near. He is waiting, listening, urging you to choose the path that leads to life, both now and for eternity.

Walk with God daily and seek His answers for your life. It's the only path that leads to real truth and satisfaction versus the lies we experience daily, which momentarily seem to provide answers but often-times lead us down a path of uncertainty and disappointment.

Let God restore your soul and encourage your heart today by seeking His daily answers to provide hope for tomorrow and beyond.

January

January 1

Enter In

"I am the LORD your God. Consecrate yourselves therefore, and be holy; for I am holy."
LEVITICUS 11:44

It is a delightful thought that whatever was symbolized by the holy of holies, whatever is its correlative and analogue in the nature of God, is ours, not to enter for a transient yearly visit, but to become our home and abiding-place.

The veil has been rent, the separation between us and the innermost fellowship with God is abolished, the way into the holiest has been made through the blood of Jesus, we are free to enter thither with all boldness, we are invited to live there forevermore.

~ F. B. Meyer

Father, You are holy and it is our desire
that we will move close to You
for fellowship with You. *Amen*

God's Throne

Draw near with confidence to the throne of grace,
so that we may receive mercy and
find grace to help in time of need.

HEBREWS 4:16

As we kneel before our now ascended Savior's throne, let us remember well the way by which He prepared it as a throne of grace for us; let us in spirit drink of His cup, that we may be strengthened for our hour of heaviness whenever it may come.

In His natural body every member suffered, and so must it be in the spiritual; but as out of all His griefs and woes His body came forth uninjured to glory and power, even so shall His mystical body come through the furnace with not so much as the smell of fire upon it.

~ Charles H. Spurgeon

God, we cannot begin to imagine what You
actually did for us so that You could, in turn,
provide a throne of grace for Your children.
Help us to draw near to You. *Amen*

The Gospel

I am not ashamed of the gospel,
for it is the power of God for salvation
to everyone who believes,
to the Jew first and also to the Greek.

ROMANS 1:16

The Gospel is for us and is instrumental in the Christian home in helping families understand Christ, their salvation, how to rear their children, how to handle business, how to be pure in relationships and every other thing we need.

The foundation of all we need is found in the Word of God. The Bible does not tell us how to plan a meal for the family or how to landscape the yard. What it does do is to show us how to be saved and teaches us how to live ... forever.

Jesus, we love You and praise
You for who You are.
We pray that we will not
be ashamed of the Gospel,
for it is life to us. *Amen*

Active Agents

He who is wise wins souls.
PROVERBS 11:30

If you are a Christian, you are the active agent through whom Christ expresses Himself. You and He are one in the great saving task, so that with Paul you can say, "It is no longer I who live, but Christ lives in me" (Gal. 2:20).

This is not to suffer the destruction of your own individuality; on the contrary, it is to have Christ energize all your creative capacities; for Christ is a living, moving, dynamic force, and He always leaves you free to work out the concrete program demanded by the need of the hour.

Thank You, Lord, for changing
me to make me like You.
May the creativity You instilled
in me be used for Your work
here on earth. *Amen*

Number One

*You will also declare a thing,
and it will be established for you;
so light will shine on your ways.*

JOB 22:28 NKJV

God intended for a man and a woman to be to one another in marriage the only love of their life. When anything comes between them that would distort in any way what God has set up, it is grievous to His heart.

The man and woman in a marriage relationship must be so committed that there is trust beyond what they can even comprehend. Jumping to conclusions is not trusting the other person and not trusting God. Spouses are a gift to us from a loving Father. Let not the romance die, but let it flourish and bud new blossoms of beauty of character, hope and love, forever.

Lord, You want us to be number one
to our spouse for as long as we both
shall live. Help us to be worthy
of such an honor. *Amen*

A Clear Conscience

If I were still trying to please men,
I would not be a bond servant of Christ.
GALATIANS 1:10

Robert C. Chapman proclaimed, "I bow to the sovereignty of God my heavenly Father; I have no will but His. We know that God is love, and if, with love of which there is no measure, there be conjoined wisdom which makes no mistakes, what becomes us, His children, but to be full of thankfulness?"

"For God, who said, 'Light shall shine out of darkness,' is the One who has shone in our hearts to give the Light of the knowledge of the glory of God in the face of Christ. But we have this treasure in earthen vessels, so that the surpassing greatness of the power will be of God and not from ourselves" (2 Cor. 4:6-7).

Lord, as I desire to please You,
only then every other situation
will fall into place. *Amen*

January 7

A Tribute

Honor her for all that her hands have done,
and let her works bring her praise at the city gate.
PROVERBS 31:31 NIV

Louisa May Alcott, in her poem *Tribute to a Mother*, so beautifully describes women who are there and who deserve praise:

Faith that withstood the shocks of toil and time;
Hope that defied despair;
Patience that conquered care;
And loyalty, whose courage was sublime;
The great deep heart that was a home for all –
Just, eloquent, and strong
In protest against wrong;
Wide charity, that knew no sin, no fall;
The Spartan spirit that made life so grand
Mating poor daily needs
With high, heroic deeds,
That wrested happiness from Fate's hard hand.

Lord, bless our mothers who have given all
they possibly could to assure our needs were
met and our hearts were introduced to You.
Bless them, indeed, we pray. *Amen*

Jesus Fulfilled the Law

"I did not come to abolish but to fulfill."
MATTHEW 5:17

Jesus came to fulfill the law and the prophets. Before He could fulfill, He had to know the law and the prophets. Jesus knew the Scriptures.

He quoted them when He was tempted in the wilderness. He used them for His inaugural message in the synagogue at Nazareth. He cited the Old Testament in the Sermon on the Mount. He quoted from the Psalms when His body was dying on the cross.

We must know the law if we are to fulfill as Christ has set forth in His living example.

As we study Your Word, may we learn it and hide it in our hearts so that we might fulfill it while we live on earth. *Amen*

January 9

Getting Rid of Guilt

*Wash away all my iniquity and
cleanse me from my sin.*

PSALM 51:2 NIV

Visiting his grandparents' farm, a boy was given a slingshot, but he struggled to hit his target so he decided to sling at his grandmother's pet duck, accidentally killing it. He hid the dead duck in the wood pile only to see his sister watching, but she said nothing. The next day Grandma said, "Sally, let's wash the dishes."

Sally said, "Johnny wants to help," as she whispered to him, *"Remember the duck?"* Johnny did the dishes! Grandpa invited the children to go fishing, but Grandma needed Sally to help make supper. Again, *"Remember the duck?"* Sally went fishing!

Several days of Johnny doing both his chores and Sally's left him unable to stand it any longer, so he confessed: "I killed the duck!" Hugging him, Grandma said, "I saw the whole thing, but because I love you, I forgave you, and I wondered how long you would let Sally make a slave of you."

Jesus, thank You for paying the sin debt
so we are no longer slaves. *Amen*

Suffering Used for Good

They cried out for help,
and their cry rose up to God.
EXODUS 2:23 NLT

Before God wrought that great deliverance for them at the Red Sea, they were brought into great distress, the wilderness had shut them in, they could not turn to the right hand nor the left, and the Red Sea was before them, and the great Egyptian host behind, and they were brought to see that they could do nothing to help themselves, and that if God did not help them, they should be immediately swallowed up; and then God appeared, and turned their cries into songs.

So before they were brought to their rest, and to enjoy the milk and honey of Canaan, God "led them through a great and terrible wilderness, that he might humble them and teach them what was in their heart, and so do them good in their latter end."

~ Jonathan Edwards

Thank You, Lord, that You teach us
in times of suffering. *Amen*

Amber Alert

For the eyes of the LORD move to
and fro throughout the earth
that He may strongly support those
whose heart is completely His.
2 CHRONICLES 16:9

A s a result of the abduction and murder of a young girl, the Amber Alert was founded and in 2003 President George W. Bush signed into law the Amber Alert Bill. Major cities across America can now sound an alarm about an abducted child, including many details to encourage citizens to help look for the child and the perpetrator.

God watches out for us, His children. What a wonderful thing to know that He loves so much that He is alert to our whereabouts.

Thank You, Lord, for watching out
for us and for guiding us in
along the way we should go. *Amen*

January 12

True Beauty

Your beauty should not come from outward adornment, such as elaborate hairstyles and the wearing of gold jewelry or fine clothes. Rather, it should be that of your inner self, the unfading beauty of a gentle and quiet spirit, which is of great worth in God's sight.

1 PETER 3:3-4 NIV

On the first of May in the olden times, according to annual custom, many inhabitants of London went into the fields to bathe their faces with the early dew upon the grass under the idea that it would render them beautiful.

Some writers call the custom superstitious; it may have been so, but this we know, that to bathe one's face every morning in the dew of heaven by prayer and communion, is the sure way to obtain true beauty of life and character.

~ Charles H. Spurgeon

Lord, help me to obtain true beauty by making time to spend with You every day. *Amen*

January 13

Binding Common Sense

Give attention to my wisdom.

PROVERBS 5:1

Leslie E. Maxwell said, "Many men are forever standing on their heads, i.e. they are depending upon their own understanding. Their self-styled common sense forever binds them, renders them spiritually impotent. They dare not venture to walk with Christ on the water because their understanding knows that no man can walk on the water.

Christ's call cannot be heard, therefore, above their common sense; they can see only disaster and drowning. Though they admit readily that Peter's cold, calculating common sense sank him, the truth is Peter's head but betrayed his unbelieving heart. Was Peter's seeing believing? Common sense may say so, but Scripture says Peter saw the winds and waves, and – sank!"

Lord, help is to not test Your resources until we attempt the impossible. *Amen*

Be Slow to Wrath

He who is slow to wrath has great understanding,
but he who is impulsive exalts folly.

PROVERBS 14:29 NKJV

Corrie ten Boom, who spent time in a Nazi concentration camp, had every reason to hate, but she said, "When we forgive we set a prisoner free — ourselves." She knew suffering most of us can't imagine and yet she chose to forgive her captors. By doing so, she knew she had been set free from the bondage of a life filled with hate and bitterness.

If bitterness is robbing you of the joy Christ has for all His children, wouldn't it be a good thing to ask for His forgiveness and then make restitution with those on your hate list? God has so much more for His young ones than to spend our lives warped because we cannot forgive.

Father, help us as Christians
to forgive. *Amen*

January 15

Believers Fellowship

Let us not neglect our meeting together,
as some people do, but encourage one another,
especially now that the day of
His return is drawing near.

HEBREWS 10:25 NLT

Worship is the submission of all of our nature to God. It is the quickening of conscience by His holiness, the nourishment of mind by His truth, the purifying of imagination by His beauty, the opening of the heart to His love, and the submission of will to His purpose. And all of this gathered up in adoration is the greatest expression of which we are capable.

~ William Temple

God, may we be so much like You
that people will see You in us
and can be ministered to by us.
Help us, we pray, to have hearts that
are so pliable in Your hands that
You can mold us to Your blueprint. *Amen*

January 16

Bible Knowledge

*And the Word became flesh, and dwelt among us,
and we beheld His glory, glory as of the only
begotten from the Father, full of grace and truth.*
JOHN 1:14

We are mistaken if we think that we can get along with slovenly and incomplete knowledge of the Bible. No amount of spiritual experience, or even the Spirit's help and instruction will take the place of the study God requires us to put upon His Word.

~ Katherine Bushnell

God, may we be on our faces seeking You and
learning about You through Your Holy Word.
Thank You for the Bible.
Thank You that the words are true.
Between its pages lie the wealth of knowledge
we need to be exactly what You want us to be
so that our lives will bring blessing,
honor and glory to the Lord. *Amen*

January 17

Blessed!

I know that when I come to you,
I will come in the fullness
of the blessing of Christ.

ROMANS 15:29

Blessed indeed are those in the kingdom of heaven, but if any seek this Kingdom with motives of self-blessing merely, they will fail to find it. Only as the eyes are turned away from self can one truly seek or see God. Jesus used the word "blessed" in pointing out those in the Kingdom, that we may know who they are; not to emphasize blessings conferred.

We should be careful how we appeal to motives of self-interest in connection with entering upon the Christian life, else we may block the way which we seek to open; for the blessed life is an unselfish life.

God, You have blessed us, and we are grateful.

May we stand against any temptation

to turn away from You. *Amen*

Brokenness

He will sit as a smelter and purifier of silver,
and He will purify the sons of Levi
and refine them like gold and silver,
so that they may present to the
LORD offerings in righteousness.

MALACHI 3:3

When Christ shall see His own image in His people, His work of purifying will be accomplished. Henri Nouwen once said, "Our life is full of brokenness – broken relationships, broken promises, broken expectations. How can we live with that brokenness without becoming bitter and resentful except by returning again and again to God's faithful presence in our lives?"

Lord Jesus, You came that we might have life.
Refine us, we pray, so that the reflection of
Your face will be seen in ours.
Make us like You, we pray. *Amen*

Breaking Point

*"When the Helper comes, whom I will send
to you from the Father, that is the
Spirit of truth who proceeds from the Father,
He will testify about Me."*

JOHN 15:26

Life is a mixture of good times and bad times, happy moments and unhappy moments. The next time you are experiencing one of those bad times or unhappy moments that take you close to your breaking point, bend but don't break. Try your best not to let the situation get the best of you. A measure of hope will take you through the unpleasant ordeal.

With hope for a better tomorrow or a better situation, things may not be as bad as they seem. Hardships may be easier to deal with if the end result is worth having.

Lord, we will call upon Your name
in the day of trouble. *Amen*

Christianity

*The disciples were first called
Christians in Antioch.*
ACTS 11:26

Thomas S. Eliot wrote, "Christ gave His all so that we can have life eternal with Him in heaven. How wonderful it is when we have some of heaven here on earth. A Christ-centered marriage is one way to do that. Is Christ Jesus the head of your home? If not, remember, He is not the one that moved away.

The greatest proof of Christianity for others is not how far a man can logically analyze his reasons for believing, but how far in practice he will stake his life on his belief."

We are humbled, Lord, by what
You did for us at Calvary.
We pray, in Your name,
that men and women will
desire You to be the head of
their homes as they serve You
in front of a lost world. *Amen*

The Work of Faith

*Ask of God, who gives to all liberally and
without reproach, and it will be given to him.
But let him ask in faith, with no doubting,
for he who doubts is like a wave of the sea
driven and tossed by the wind.*

JAMES 1:5-6 NKJV

It was Thomas who said, "Where reason cannot wade there faith may swim." Faith, when allowed to do the work God ordained it to do, will take off with speed. We, then, can enjoy the beauty of the white caps as they move off to the horizon. Trusting in God in every circumstance is the ultimate of faith.

~ David Dickson

Father, help us to look to You,
the author and finisher of our faith. *Amen*

January 22

Life Is a Process

LORD, make me to know my end
And what is the extent of my days;
let me know how transient I am.

PSALM 39:4

George Washington Carver said, "How far you go in life depends on your being tender with the young, compassionate with the aged, sympathetic with the striving, and tolerant of the weak and the strong. Because someday in life you will have been all of these."

Precious Lord, there is truly a time for everything.
Help us to grow in Your grace with each phase
and help us to allow You to be our guide
as we reach out to those around us.
May our lives be a joy to You. *Amen*

January 23

Liberty! Oh, Yes!

It was for freedom that Christ set us free.
GALATIANS 5:1

On March 23, 1775, Patrick Henry said, "It is in vain, sir, to extenuate the matter. Gentlemen may cry, 'Peace, Peace' – but there is no peace. The war is actually begun! The next gale that sweeps from the north will bring to our ears the clash of resounding arms! Our brethren are already in the field!

Why stand we here idle? What is it that gentlemen wish? What would they have? Is life so dear, or peace so sweet, as to be purchased at the price of chains and slavery? Forbid it, Almighty God! I know not what course others may take; but as for me, give me liberty or give me death!"

O God, how blessed we are to have liberty,

though at the expense of countless lives lost for it.

Thank You for our liberty as Christians.

Death has no victory over Your children. *Amen*

Build Up or Destroy?

"Blessed are the pure in heart, for they shall see God."
MATTHEW 5:8

I watched them tearing a building down, a gang of men in a busy town; with a ho-heave-ho and a lusty yell they swung a beam and the sidewalk fell. I asked the foreman: "Are these men skilled, and the men you'd hire if you had to build?" He gave me a laugh and said: "No indeed! Just common labor is all I need. I can easily wreck in a day or two what builders have taken a year to do!"

And I thought to myself as I went my way, which of these roles have I tried to play?

Am I a builder who works with care, measuring a life by the rule and square? Am I shaping my deeds to a well-made plan, patiently doing the best I can? Or am I a wrecker, who walks the town, content with the labor of tearing down.

Lord God, help us to be about Your business here on earth of winning the lost and of building our Christian siblings up in the faith. *Amen*

January 25

My Safe Place

God has said, "I will never fail you.
I will never abandon you."
HEBREWS 13:5 NLT

I used to have a comfort zone where I knew I wouldn't fail. The same four walls and busy work were really more like jail. I longed so much to do the things I'd never done before, but stayed inside my comfort zone and paced the same old floor.

I said it didn't matter that I wasn't doing much. I said I didn't care for things like commission checks and such. I claimed to be so busy with things inside my zone, but deep inside I longed for something special of my own. I couldn't let my life go by just watching others win.

I held my breath; I stepped outside and let the change begin. I took a step and with new strength I'd never felt before, I kissed my comfort zone goodbye and closed and locked the door.

Father, You are our safe place. *Amen*

The Spirit of Truth

*"When the Spirit of truth comes,
He will guide you into all truth."*

JOHN 16:13 NLT

Truth may be compared to some cave or grotto, with wondrous stalactites hanging from the roof, and others starting from the floor; a cavern glittering with spar and abounding in marvels.

Before entering the cavern you enquire for a guide, who comes with his lighted flambeau. He leads you through different chambers. Here he points you to a little stream rushing from amid the rocks, and indicates its rise and progress ... then takes you into a large natural hall, tells you how many persons once feasted in it, and so on.

Truth is a grand series of caverns, it is our glory to have so great and wise a conductor as the Holy Spirit. Imagine that we are coming to the darkness of it. He is a light shining in the midst of us to guide us. And by the light he shows us wondrous things.

~ Charles H. Spurgeon

Spirit of God, guide me in the
Truth to where I need to be. *Amen*

Godly Contentment

Not that I speak from want,
for I have learned to be content
in whatever circumstances I am.

PHILIPPIANS 4:11

Instead of complaining at his lot, a contented man is thankful that his condition and circumstances are no worse than they are. Instead of greedily desiring something more than the supply of his present need, he rejoices that God still cares for him. Such an one is 'content' with such as he has.

~ A. R. Pink

Help us, Lord, to know contentment

and to live so that others might

come to know the same peace

that comes only from knowing

and trusting You for our

daily supply. *Amen*

Continuous Conversion

Be transformed
by the renewing of your mind.
ROMANS 12:2

The hindrance in our spiritual life is that we will not be continually converted, there are wedges of obstinacy where our pride spits at the throne of God and says – I won't. We deify independence and willfulness and call them by the wrong name. What God looks on as obstinate weakness, we call strength.

There are whole tracts of our lives which have not yet been brought into subjection, and it can only be done by this continuous conversion. Slowly but surely we can claim the whole territory for the Spirit of God.

~ Oswald Chambers

Savior, help us to continually
be transformed by the
renewing of our minds. *Amen*

Delivered by His Hand

He will deliver the needy.

PSALM 72:12

"For He shall deliver the needy ... and him that hath no helper." Do not be too afraid of getting into the spot where you have no helper, for that is the spot where, like Jacob, you will meet a delivering God. Do not be too anxious to be free from needs, unless you want to be free from prayer power. Accept them just as God sends them or permits them.

The moment you come to a need, remember also that you have come to a promise. "He shall deliver the needy." To miss a need may be to miss a miracle. As soon as one appears in your life, do not begin to worry because it is there, but praise God because it is to be supplied.

Father, thank You for meeting every need we have. *Amen*

Discipline and Order

*He who neglects discipline
despises himself.*
PROVERBS 15:32

"We are apt to forget," wrote Oswald Chambers, "that a man is not only committed to Jesus Christ for salvation; he is committed to Jesus Christ's view of God, of the world, of sin, and of the devil, and this will mean that he must recognize the responsibility of being transformed by the renewing of his mind."

Father God, we pray that You would
help us to remember that You are a God
of order and discipline.
We are reminded that in the beginning,
You never started a new task until
You completed the one You were working on.
Thank You for the lessons You teach us
in such gracious and kind ways. *Amen*

The Music of Eternity

Now faith is the assurance of things hoped for,
the conviction of things not seen.

HEBREWS 11:1

Faith is not blind acceptance of absurdity. Faith is the completion of a transaction in which we submit ourselves to a personal relationship with an unseen and living Master. Faith is such an adventure as every sailor makes when he sets out for an unseen port.

Faith is our response to our yearning for the God who has made us for fellowship with Him. Faith is the answer of the vibrant human spirit to the music of eternity. Christians need faith as we walk with Christ and as we tend to everything about us.

Lord God, we pray that, in faith,
we will respond to Your perfect
will for our lives. *Amen*

February

February 1

True Love

Love never fails.
1 CORINTHIANS 13:8

Søren Kierkegaard said, "To the Christian, love is the works of love. To say that love is a feeling or anything of the kind is really an unchristian conception of love. That is the aesthetic definition and therefore fits the erotic and everything of that nature. But to the Christian, love is the works of love. Christ's love was not an inner feeling, a full heart and whatnot: it was the work of love which was His life."

And John 3:16 tells us, "For God so loved the world, that He gave His only begotten Son, that whoever believes in Him shall not perish, but have eternal life." That is the ultimate love.

God, thank You for the love
we can have for others.
How loving You are, Father,
to teach us how to love,
and how to accept love. *Amen*

Tend to the Sheep!

Another angel came out of the temple,
crying out with a loud voice,
"The hour to reap has come,
because the harvest of the earth is ripe."
REVELATION 14:15

While modern-day technological conveniences are necessities for most of us, the other side is often lacking: Most of us are so involved going about the business of managing these modern machines that we have little or no time for people.

God certainly wants us to take care of what He has blessed us with, but He did not put us here to cater to the gadgets that are a part of our daily lives. We are here to spread the gospel to the lost world around us. When we are too busy for people, we are too busy! Perhaps we should rethink turning on another machine until we go out and tend to some of the sheep!

Father, help us to use our time to bear witness of You in our lives. *Amen*

February 3

Single Moms

Who can find a virtuous and capable wife?
PROVERBS 31:10 NLT

The needs of the single mom are great. Even when there are no financial needs, which is the exception, there are thousands of other needs. God obviously has allowed for single mothers to be a part of this world because the Bible talks about widows and unwed mothers. These women are dear to the very heart of God.

Father, God, we pray for the single moms
of this world and ask that You would bring
godly relationships to them through
their churches and through their communities.
Lord, help each of us to pay attention to the
ways You want us to minister to the needs
of lonely and hurting single moms.
Help them to draw near to Your heart for
comfort, care and guidance.
Bless them and their children. *Amen*

February 4

Are You Prepared?

Jesus' disciples asked Him,
"Where do You want us to go and
make preparations for You to eat the Passover?"

MARK 14:12 NIV

The greater a work that a man undertakes, the more important is the preparation. Four days before the Passover the Israelite had to make his preparations. The Lord Jesus also desired that care should be taken to obtain an upper room furnished and ready where the Passover might be prepared.

When I am called upon to meet my God and to sit down at His table, I will see to it that I do not approach it unprepared. Otherwise I should dishonor Him and lose the blessing which is destined for me, and cover my soul with heavy guilt.

~ Andrew Murray

God, may we be prepared
at all times to dine with You,
for we never know when You
will call us home to our
heavenly feast. *Amen*

A Life Poured Out

He gave up His divine privileges;
He took the humble position of a slave
and was born as a human being.

PHILIPPIANS 2:7 NLT

The soul cannot come to ... rest and contentment in Christ ... without great purity ... The new mantle which belonged to the betrothal could not be put on until the old mantle was stripped off.

Wherefore, he that refuses to go forth in the night aforementioned to seek the Beloved, and to be stripped of his own will and to be mortified, but seeks Him upon his bed and at his own convenience, as did the Bride, will not succeed in finding Him. For this soul says of itself that it found Him by going forth in the dark and with yearnings of love.

~ St. John of the Cross

Father, our hearts desire
that our lives will be instrumental
in helping the lost to find You. *Amen*

February 6

Teaching through Prayer

"He who has ears to hear, let him hear!"
LUKE 8:8 NKJV

If religion teaches us anything concerning eating and drinking, or spending our time and money; if it teaches us how we are to use the world; if it tells us what tempers we are to have in common life, how we are to be disposed towards all people: how we are to behave towards the sick, the poor, the old, the destitute; if it tells us whom we are to treat with a particular love, whom we are to regard with a particular esteem; if it tells us how we are to treat our enemies, and how we are to mortify and deny ourselves; he must be very weak that can think these parts of religion are not to be observed with as much exactness, as any doctrines that relate to prayers.

~ William Law

Help us, Lord, to listen with our hearts
to all You have for us to learn. *Amen*

His Will Alone!

I delight to do Your will, O My God.

PSALM 40:8

We must literally use our own will to turn our hearts to make the decisions of God's will. It is not so easy for us when the world, with all its excitement, ease and momentary thrills pulls us in different directions. Of course, the world rarely, if ever, shows the true or the whole picture. Most often the end of that direction is distorted or not even in view at all.

The Bible says the way of the world leads to destruction. When we seek His will and objectively accept it, no matter our present circumstances, there is freedom and surety in that decision.

Lord, thank You for providing
all we need to live out the plans
You have for our lives. *Amen*

Finding Forgiveness

There is forgiveness with You.

PSALM 130:4 NKJV

I will place you on my lap and wipe away your tears. Then, I will smile. A smile to let you know I am pleased. For when you're hurt and when you've sinned, still, you came to Me. So, do not draw back from Me, my child, I am Abba Father to you; remember in My Word, I said, "Behold, I make all things new."

I will forgive you, heal you, restore you, I will shower you with grace. I will never turn My back to you, but you will see My face. On your journey home, when I see you I will run ... Even if, even if, My child, even if just come.

Dear God, You have taught us how to forgive.

I pray that we will forgive those who wrong us,

and forget that wrong. *Amen*

February 9

True Friends

A friend loves at all times.
PROVERBS 17:17 NIV

Everyone hears what you say. Friends listen to what you say. Best friends listen to what you don't say. A friend is someone who knows the song in your heart and can sing it back to you when you have forgotten the words.

The Bible says that a real friend loves at all times — without questions or evaluations. A real friend goes beyond what most of us ever expect; they hope for the best in every area of our lives. They desire God's highest for us. Awesome!

Thank You, Father, for friends
who only want for us what
is in line with Your will.
Bless them, we pray. *Amen*

February 10

From One to Two

Two are better than one because they
have a good return for their labor.
For if either of them falls,
the one will lift up his companion.
But woe to the one who falls
when there is not another to lift him up.
ECCLESIASTES 4:9-10

Marriage is a beautiful and holy institution that God created for a man and a woman to become one, to replenish the earth, to be an example of the Bride of Christ, the church.

Such a lovely and cherished thing as marriage should never be destroyed by allowing sin to make a mockery of it. Let marriage be held in honor among all.

Lord, thank You for marriage.
I pray that we will understand the way
You designed marriage and that we
will honor Your design. *Amen*

Get Ready!
Get Set! Wait!

The end of a matter is better than its beginning.
ECCLESIASTES 7:8

If, when God sends judgments upon others, we do not take warning and example by them; if instead of reflecting upon ourselves and questioning our ways we fall to censuring others; if we will pervert the meaning of God's providences and will not understand the design and intention of them; then we leave God no other way to awaken us to a consideration of our evil ways but by pouring down His wrath upon our heads, so that He may convince us that we are sinners by the same argument from whence we have concluded others to be so.

~ John Tillotson

Lord, we do not want to interfere with
the work of the Holy Spirit in anyone's life.
Help us to wait for Your instructions. *Amen*

Blessed Giving

*"It is more blessed
to give than to receive."*

ACTS 20:35

The kingdom of God can never be established by raising money; but it can never be extended *without* raising money. To have is to owe, not to own. Truth is more eloquent lived than spoken. A man says, "This world owes me a living." He should say, "I owe the world a life."

Jean-Jacques Rousseau said, "Every man is born free." I venture to say, every individual is born in debt. We succeed to an inheritance of enormous value. God will not refuse the poor offerings of the poor, but neither will He accept the poor offerings of the rich.

Lord, it has been said that a person's
ability to do big things increases
as they prove themselves
faithful in little things. *Amen*

February 13

No Limitations
with God

*"If any of you wants to be My follower,
you must give up your own way,
take up your cross, and follow Me.
If you try to hang on to your life, you will lose it.
But if you give up your life for My sake,
you will save it."*

MATTHEW 16:24-25 NLT

Emerson said, "If you would lift me up you must be on higher ground."

Nothing is as real as a dream. The world can change around you, but your dream will not. Responsibilities need not erase it. Duties need not obscure it. Because the dream is within you, no one can take it away.

Winston Churchill said, "Kites rise highest against the wind – not with it."

Help us to see there are
no limitations with You,
O Lord. *Amen*

February 14

God's Grace

"My grace is sufficient for you."
2 CORINTHIANS 12:9

The late Thomas Watson wrote, "The Kingdom of grace is nothing but ... the beginning of the Kingdom of glory; the Kingdom of grace is glory in the seed, and the Kingdom of glory is grace in the flower; the Kingdom of grace is glory in the daybreak, and the Kingdom of glory is grace in the full meridian; the Kingdom of grace is glory militant, and the Kingdom of glory is grace triumphant ... the Kingdom of grace leads to the Kingdom of glory."

God of Grace, we bow before Your throne,

thanking You for this provision

that comes from Your heart

of love to Your children.

Help us, we pray, to recognize and

appreciate Your grace in our lives,

in our homes and in our marriages. *Amen*

February 15

God's Voice

The unfolding of Your words gives light;
it gives understanding to the simple.

PSALM 119:130

The Bible is the written Word of God, and because it is written it is confined and limited by the necessities of ink and paper and leather. The voice of God, however, is alive and free as the sovereign God is free.

"The words that I speak unto you, they are spirit and they are life." The life is in the speaking words. God's Word in the Bible can have power only because it corresponds to God's word in the universe. It is the present voice which makes the written Word all-powerful.

~ A. W. Tozer

Thank You for giving us Your Word, God.
Your Word is final.
Please woo us to Your heart
through its pages and keep us
strong and mighty.
We pray that we will meditate
on it day and night. *Amen*

February 16

True Repentance

*"For what profit is it to a man if he
gains the whole world, and loses his own soul?
Or what will a man give in exchange for his soul?"*

MATTHEW 16:26 NKJV

O merciful God, it is owing to Thy love and long-suffering that I lie not already in hell. I yield my *self*, with my whole will, senses and mind, unto Thy grace, and fly to Thy mercy. I call upon Thee through Thy death, from that small spark of life in me encompassed with death and hell, which open their throat against me, and would wholly swallow me up in death; upon Thee I call, Who hast promised that Thou wilt not quench the smoking flax. I have no other way to Thee but by Thy own bitter death and passion, because Thou hast made our death to be life by Thy humanity, and broken the chains of death, and therefore I sink the desire of my soul down into Thy death, into the gate of Thy death, which Thou hast broke open.

~ Jacob Boehme

"O Thou great fountain of the Love of God,
I beseech Thee, help me, that I may
die from my vanity and sin in the death of my
Redeemer, Jesus Christ" (Jacob Boehme). *Amen*

February 17

Growth in Grace

We all, with unveiled face, beholding as in a mirror
the glory of the Lord, are being transformed
into the same image from glory to glory,
just as from the Lord, the Spirit.
2 CORINTHIANS 3:18

God's children improve all advantages to advance their grand end; they labor to grow better by blessings and crosses, and to make sanctified use of all things ... if believers decay in their first love, or in some other grace, yet another grace may grow an increase, such as humility, their broken heartedness; they sometimes seem not to grow in the branches when they may grow at the root; upon a check grace breaks out more; as we say, after a hard winter there usually follows a glorious spring.

~ Richard Sibbes

Help us, Father, as we grow in grace,
to keep our hearts and minds clean
so that we will grow stronger. *Amen*

February 18

The Established Heart

It is good that the heart be established by grace, not with foods which have not profited those who have been occupied with them.

HEBREWS 13:9 NKJV

The greatest cities of human greatness have not continued ... Buried in mounds, on which grass grows luxuriantly. But, amid all, there is arising from age to age a permanent structure, an enduring City, a confederation which gathers around the unchanging Savior. Do we enough live in this City in our habitual experience? It is possible to tread its golden streets as we plod along the thoroughfares of earth's great cities; to mingle in its blessed companies, and share its holy exercises, though apparently we spend our days in dark city offices, and amid money-loving companions. The true pilgrim to the City really lives in the City. It will not be long, and it shall not be only an object for faith and spiritual vision, it shall become manifest.

~ F. B. Meyer

"The holy City out of heaven from God, radiant with His light, the metropolis of a redeemed earth, the Bride of the Lamb, for whom the universe was made" (F. B. Meyer). *Amen*

February 19

Tending the Garden

*God is not the author of confusion
but of peace.*
1 CORINTHIANS 14:33 NKJV

We are told in 1 John, "For this purpose was the Son of God made manifest to destroy the works of the devil." And Jesus verified this by word and deed.

Everything had been created by His Father-nature in all aspects, nature which He loved and which fed and refreshed His spirit; the human mind, the human spirit, even the bodies of men. Anything destructive of any part of His Father's handiwork was the work of the devil and was not to be tolerated an instant longer than necessary. The Kingdom is always constructive.

~ Catherine Marshall

Thank You, Father, for helping us to understand
the importance of all You created.
May we always be about
Your business as we tend the garden
and feed the sheep. *Amen*

February 20

His Word Our Authority

Faith comes from hearing,
and hearing by the word of Christ.
ROMANS 10:17

We are to believe and follow Christ in all things, including His words about Scripture. And this means that Scripture is to be for us what it was to Him: the unique, authoritative, and inerrant Word of God, and not merely a human testimony to Christ, however carefully guided and preserved by God. If the Bible is less than this to us, we are not fully Christ's disciples.

~ James Montgomery Boice

We have Your Word on the matter,
Lord God. Thank You,
for it is our authority. *Amen*

February 21

Love for Mothers

He said to the disciple,
"Behold, your mother!"

JOHN 19:27

Henry Wadsworth Longfellow, the famous poet, is quoted as saying that, "Even He that died for us upon the cross, in the last hour, in the unutterable agony of death, was mindful of His mother, as if to teach us that this holy love should be our last worldly thought – the last point of earth from which the soul should take its flight for heaven."

The Bible has a lot to say about mothers because mothers are precious to the heart of God.

Heavenly Father, we pray that our hearts
will join with Yours as we consider
the women who are mothers.
Grant that womanhood may be
consecrated to You, O Lord. *Amen*

February 22

Superhero Samson

The LORD is my strength and my shield.
PSALM 28:7

When Samson turned from God, he lost every-thing he had. All left him, but the Lord accepted him when he came back in repentance. When Samson returned, he looked normal physically, and his source of strength could not be determined; those around him had to ask him where he got his strength. He had a secret!

The Lord was his strength – the Spirit gave him supernatural power. Even though we may not look or appear to be anything or anyone special, God can do with us whatever He likes. He is not hindered if we belong fully to Him.

May we always recognize that the
source of our strength is You,
O Lord God. *Amen*

February 23

Have Heart

Trust in the LORD with all your heart
and do not lean on your own understanding.
In all your ways acknowledge Him,
and He will make your paths straight.
PROVERBS 3:5-6

President George W. Bush, while campaigning for the Republican primaries (in February 2000) made a very profound statement, more intellectually brilliant than many of the theologians, philosophers and politicians that have been studied for the past forty years.

When asked by reporters, "Whom do you consider the greatest philosopher?" he answered, "Christ. He changed my heart!" "For I am not ashamed of the gospel" (Rom. 1:16).

God, we love You and we ask Your forgiveness

for not always acting in the way we should.

We pray that You, Holy Father,

will help us not to be ashamed of You. *Amen*

The Vine and the Branches

"Without Me you can do nothing."
JOHN 15:5 NKJV

Nothing? That seems a trifle sweeping. Perhaps Jesus meant simply that we shall be more effective with His help than without it. But when we go back to the context in which the statement is made, we find that Jesus meant precisely what He said.

This is the allegory of the vine and the branches: "I am the vine, you are the branches." The point is not that the branches will do better when they are attached to the vine. Unless attached, the branches must wither and die.

~ Catherine Marshall

Lord Jesus, You have provided a means for
Your children to be nourished with all we need to
live the Christian life the way You intended.
Help us to draw from that never-ending supply
so we can bring honor to Your name. *Amen*

Great Leadership

"He who rules over men righteously,
who rules in the fear of God,
is as the light of the morning
when the sun rises,
a morning without clouds,
when the tender grass springs out of the earth,
through sunshine after rain."

2 SAMUEL 23:3-5

Godly leaders have a tremendous responsibility to be like Christ in all their dealings," wrote Jim Rohn. "A good objective of leadership is to help those who are doing poorly to do well and to help those who are doing well to do even better."

God, we pray that You would instill in
our religious and political leaders
an awareness of the Christian
heritage of our nation,
and the love and knowledge of God,
which is the beginning of
the making of a great leader. *Amen*

Surrender Your Will

For the weapons of our warfare
are not of the flesh,
but divinely powerful
for the destruction of fortresses.
2 CORINTHIANS 10:4

L ike any other sin, the stronghold is in the will, and the will or purpose to doubt must be surrendered exactly as you surrender the will or purpose to yield to any other temptation.

God always takes possession of a surrendered will; and if we come to the point of saying that we will doubt, and surrender this central fortress of our nature to Him, His blessed Spirit will begin at once to "work in us all the good pleasure of His will," and we shall find ourselves kept from doubting by His mighty and overcoming power.

~ Hannah Whitall Smith

Dear God, we need to be aware of

strongholds in every area of our lives and

to fortify our hearts so we will not yield to sin.

Help us not to be deceived by the enemy. *Amen*

February 27

Spiritual Vitamins

"These words which I command you ...
you shall teach them
diligently to your children."
DEUTERONOMY 6:6-7 NKJV

Catherine Marshall wrote, "Last week I produced a 'vitamin box' of dozens of favorite passages for my family. I used a concordance and looked up words such as strength, food, bread, water, hunger, and thirst. Other cards were culled from Christ's own words. Now before blessing the food at each meal, we pass the box, and one of the children chooses a card to read aloud. The nourishment is most effective when the life-giving words of Scripture are memorized and so become the permanent possessions of mind and heart."

Father, as we take in the physical nourishment

necessary for us to live each day,

help us to also take in the

spiritual nourishment necessary

to live the Christian life.

May we stay aware of the need to

replenish both daily. *Amen*

February 28

Religion in the Soul

We know that the Son of God
has come and has given us an understanding.
1 JOHN 5:20 NKJV

When we look around us and consider the characters and pursuits of men … many of them shamefully neglect it. And whatever different notions people may entertain of what they call religion, all must agree in owning that it is very far from being a universal thing.

Religion, in its most general view, is such a sense of God in the soul, and such a conviction of our obligations to Him, and of our dependence upon Him, as shall engage us to make it our great care to conduct ourselves in a manner which we have reason to believe will be pleasing to Him.

~ Philip Doddridge

"O blessed God, [may] everlasting
honors be ascribed to the Father"
(Philip Doddridge). *Amen*

March

March 1

The Answer to Loneliness

The LORD will personally go ahead of you.
He will be with you;
He will neither fail you nor abandon you.

DEUTERONOMY 31:8 NLT

Jesus is the answer to loneliness! He has promised to be our burden bearer and He said He will wipe away all our tears (see Rev. 21:4). He wants us to find joy and happiness in Him.

By doing so, we can become acquainted with His peace that takes the sting out of certain times of loneliness. He puts contentment in place of the fear of being alone. He is just a prayer away.

Jesus, it is so very comforting to know
that You are always with us.
No matter how afraid we are,
or what circumstances we are in,
You will not forsake us.
Thank You, Lord, for Your Word
that is so reassuring. *Amen*

Humble Us

Before honor comes humility.
PROVERBS 15:33

God's children are strengthened by their falls; they learn to stand by their falls. Like tall cedars, the more they are blown the deeper they will be rooted.

That which men think is the overthrow of God's children does but root them the deeper, so that after all outward storms and inward declensions this is the issue, 'They take root downward and bear fruit upward' for the Lord restores their souls.

~ Richard Sibbes

Father, we pray that You
would make us humble people.
You exemplify humility.
Help us to learn at Your feet. *Amen*

The Call of God

We are His workmanship,
created in Christ Jesus for good works,
which God prepared beforehand
so that we would walk in them.

EPHESIANS 2:10

George Campbell Morgan said, "God has foreordained the works to which He has called you. He has been ahead of you preparing the place to which you are coming and manipulating all the resources of the universe in order that the work you do may be a part of His whole great and gracious work."

Lord, help us to clearly know Your voice and to follow it always. *Amen*

Loving Affection

Love is patient and kind.
Love is not jealous or boastful or proud or rude.
It does not demand its own way.
1 CORINTHIANS 13:4-5 NLT

Nathaniel Hawthorne said, "Caresses, expressions of one sort or another, are necessary to the life of the affections as leaves are to the life of a tree. If they are wholly restrained, love will die at the roots."

Some years later, Longfellow wrote, "Talk not of wasted affection. Affection never was wasted."

Father, You have taught us how to
be affectionate and how to love.
Thank You for loving relationships
here on earth and for the love relationship
Your children enjoy with You. *Amen*

March 5

Loving Discipline

*No chastening seems to be joyful for the present,
but painful; nevertheless, afterward it yields
the peaceable fruit of righteousness
to those who have been trained by it.*

HEBREWS 12:11 NKJV

Discipline is not God's way of saying, "I'm through with you," or a mark of abandonment. Rather, it is the loving act of God to bring us back. C. S. Lewis said, "God whispers to us in our pleasure; He speaks to us in our work; He shouts at us in our pain."

Someone once wrote, "Every one of us knows that there have been times when we would not listen to God or pay any attention to what His Word was saying, until finally He used a severe discipline to get our attention."

Father God, help us to understand why
discipline is vital to our growth as Christians.
We love You, Lord. *Amen*

Thank You for the Memories

To You, O LORD, I will sing praises.

PSALM 101:1

As I look back on my life I find myself wondering ... Did I remember to thank you for all that you have done for me? For all of the times you were by my side to help me celebrate my successes and accept my defeats? Or for teaching me the value of hard work, good judgment, courage, and honesty?

I wonder if I've ever thanked you for the simple things ... the laughter, the smiles, and the quiet times we've shared? If I have forgotten to, express my gratitude for any of these things, I am thanking you now ... and hoping that you've known all along, how very much you are loved and appreciated.

Lord, thank You for the privilege

of loving and for giving thanks

for loved ones who serve You. *Amen*

God's Will for Our Lives

"Come now, and let us reason together,"
says the LORD.
ISAIAH 1:18

Whether desire and will, and whether prefer-ence and volition be precisely the same things, I trust it will be allowed by all, that in every act of will there is an act of *choice;* that in every volition there is a *preference*, or a prevailing inclination of the soul, whereby at that instant, it is out of a state of perfect indifference, with respect to the direct object of the volition. So that in every act, or going forth of the will; there is some preponderation of the mind.

~ Jonathan Edwards

We pray, Lord God, that we will reason
together with You and know Your desire
and Your will for our lives. *Amen*

March 8

Lives That Honor God

If anyone cleanses himself ...
he will be a vessel for honor,
sanctified and useful for the Master,
prepared for every good work.
2 TIMOTHY 2:21 NKJV

There is but one straight road to success and that is merit. The man who is successful is the man who is useful. Capacity never lacks opportunity. It cannot remain undiscovered, because it is sought by too many anxious to use it" (B. Cockran).

Christ knows the worth in every person He created. He has praise for His children when we commit to Him and strive to be like Him on earth. He is always available to cover us with His merit badge of excellence when we live for Him.

Your love is awesome, Lord, and we
want to be so much in tune to
Your ways so that our lives
will bring honor to You. *Amen*

March 9

Purity and Modesty

Train the younger women to love their husbands
and their children, to live wisely and be pure.

TITUS 2:4-5 NLT

True modesty is the highest grace and adornment of womanhood. Modesty is the daughter of chastity; and wherever the heart is clean, true modesty is sure to reside.

A most desirable lack in our modern life is that of true modesty in both men and women. The first of all virtues is innocence; the next, modesty. If we banish modesty out of the world, she carries away with her half the virtue that is in it.

Our bodies belong to You, dear God.
Help us to adorn ourselves with modesty
so that we may set examples for the young people
we are to teach and so that You will be blessed
by our appearance. *Amen*

March 10

The Value of Mothers

Her worth is far above jewels.
PROVERBS 31:10

No amount of money could compensate for what our mothers have done for us. Mothers have held families together for years with little more than threads of love. Some mothers have a much more difficult life than others, but God makes no mistakes and He perfectly fits us together with the mother of His choosing.

Mothers are to be revered with honor. How wonderful it will be when they stand before Christ and our mothers are praised before the host in heaven for who they are. Hallelujah!

Father, thank You for mothers.
I pray that we will honor them daily
by showing our love and appreciation
for who they are. *Amen*

March 11

Mothers-In-Law

Then Naomi her mother-in-law said to her,
"My daughter, shall I not seek security for you,
that it may be well with you?"

RUTH 3:1

When Ruth's husband died, Naomi, his mother who had a precious relationship with her daughter-in-law, offered Ruth wise counsel and help with an abundance of love and honor.

The Book of Ruth is a loving example of their Christ-centered relationship. Our mothers-in-law are to be respected and honored. Without them, we would not be blessed with the gift of our spouses.

Thank You, Lord, for our mothers-in-law.
To have another godly woman we can call Mom
is a gift to be cherished. Bless these women who so
lovingly raised the people we married. *Amen*

Sacrificial Offering

"I will put enmity between you and the woman,
and between your seed and her seed."

GENESIS 3:15

Abel's sacrifice was more excellent than that of Cain, because he offered it up in faith of the promised Messiah and His suffering work, the antitype of all sacrifices.

Cain evidently scoffed at the promise or at least ignored it and offered his sacrifice apart from its faith, provisions and typical meaning. He rejected the Gospel, and sought to come to God another way, in himself and his own works, rather than a substitute, the Messiah, God's provision.

The Messiah was promised to the seed of Abraham … "In thy seed shall all the families of the earth be blessed."

~ N. V. Williams

Lord, thank You for our
rich spiritual heritage. *Amen*

Motto for Life

My son, give attention to my words;
incline your ear to my sayings.
Do not let them depart from your sight;
keep them in the midst of your heart.

PROVERBS 4:20-21

Christians have, at some time, written on the walls of our hearts the motto: "I will strive to do what Jesus would have me to do." Few will question the sincerity of this profession when our daily living shows us trying to follow this motto.

However, if we habitually absent ourselves from the church, fail to devote time and means to the kingdom's work, and disregard the motto which, as a Christian, we should be following, we soon become known for who we really are — Christians in name only with a splendid motto hung on the wall, but not practiced.

Lord, I pray that my standard for life
will always be Your Holy Word. *Amen*

Consistent Actions

*Walk in love, just as Christ also loved you,
and gave Himself up for us,
an offering and a sacrifice
to God as a fragrant aroma.*

EPHESIANS 5:2

It's not what we do once in a while that counts, but our consistent actions. And what is the father of all action? What ultimately determines who we become and where we go in life?

The answer is our decisions. It's in these moments that our destiny is shaped. More than anything else, I believe our decisions – not the conditions of our lives – determine our destiny.

~ Anthony Robbins

Lord Jesus, help us to take care of our character and to not allow our own self-interest to take root and develop into anger. *Amen*

My Shepherd

The LORD is my shepherd ...
PSALM 23:1

The Lord is my Shepherd! God loves us so much that He is willing to shepherd us throughout our Christian lives. He, as our Shepherd, is so concerned about us that He watches over us, blesses us, loves us, and even laid down His life for ours. He sees value and worth in us and He encourages us to be strong and mighty, like Him, and to spend eternity with Him in Paradise.

Imagine that, He wants us in Paradise – with HIM! How humbling to think of God, who is our Shepherd. All He asks of us is that we follow! Follow Him, the Good Shepherd.

Father, I am so thankful You are my Shepherd.

I pray that I will willingly follow You

all the days of my life. *Amen*

March 16

No Magic in Prayer

"It shall come to pass that before they call, I will answer; and while they are still speaking, I will hear."
ISAIAH 65:24 NKJV

Even if all the things that people prayed for happened – which they do not – this would not prove what Christians mean by the efficacy of prayer. For prayer is request. The essence of request, as distinct from compulsion, is that it may or may not be granted. And if an infinitely wise Being listens to the requests of finite and foolish creatures, of course He will sometimes grant and sometimes refuse them.

Invariable "success" in prayer would not prove the Christian doctrine at all. It would prove something more like magic – a power in certain human beings to control, or compel, the course of nature.

~ C. S. Lewis

Father, thank You for the gift of prayer
and that You are always willing to listen
to the longings of our hearts. *Amen*

March 17

Altogether Lovely

Let the high praises of God be in their mouth.
PSALM 149:6 NKJV

Is Jesus Christ altogether lovely? Then I beseech you set your souls upon this lovely Jesus. I am sure such an object as has been here represented, would compel love from the coldest breast and hardest heart.

Away with those empty nothings, away with this vain deceitful world, which deserves not the thousandth part of the love you give it. Let all stand aside and give way to Christ. Oh if only you knew His worth and excellency, what He is in Himself, what He has done for you, and deserved from you, you would need no arguments of mine to persuade you to love Him!

~ John Flavel

Lord, may praises to You be
on our lips and in our hearts every
moment of every day. *Amen*

March 18

Parent and Friend

Your eyes are open to all the ways of the sons of men,
to give everyone according to his ways
and according to the fruit of his doings.

JEREMIAH 32:19 NKJV

Life is not always rosy for parents and their children. Some relationships go through frightful times and long separations are a part of these when they are at their lowest.

God is always there to heal the wounded and brokenhearted. He wants the relationship between parent and child to be as Christlike as they can be. This is not easy, especially in the world we live in today. However, God has shown us His will and taught us how to accomplish His will in His Word and through prayer.

Thank You, Father,
for parents who are
also friends. *Amen*

March 19

Silence Is Golden

My soul waits in silence for God.
PSALM 62:1

Silence promotes the presence of God, prevents many harsh and proud words, and suppresses many dangers in the way of ridiculing or harshly judging our neighbors ...

If you are faithful in keeping silent when it is not necessary to speak, God will preserve you from evil when it is right for you to talk.

~ François Fénelon

Lord, You went away to pray and
we need time to be alone with You.
Make us aware of the importance
of silence so we can hear the still
small voice of God. *Amen*

March 20

All to Jesus

Into Your hand I commit my spirit;
You have ransomed me,
O Lord, God of truth.

PSALM 31:5

All things are safe in Jehovah's hands; what we entrust to the Lord will be secure, both now and in that day of days towards which we are hastening. It is peaceful living, and glorious dying, to repose in the care of heaven.

At all times we should commit our all to Jesus' faithful hand; then, though life may hang on a thread, and adversities may multiply as the sands of the sea, our soul shall dwell at ease, and delight itself in quiet resting places.

~ Charles H. Spurgeon

Giving all to You, Lord Jesus,

is what we need to do.

As we desire to know that kind of rest,

we ask that You teach us Your

ways and Your truth. *Amen*

Honoring Mothers

"Honor your father and mother."
This is the first commandment with a promise.

EPHESIANS 6:2 NLT

Everyone has a mother and most of us agree that God gave us the very best in the world. A mother's role reaches so far from one end of the spectrum to the other that there is no way to describe all of her attributes.

We may not be able to count all the ways they are so dear to us, but we can show them our love and tenderness by being the very best child for them that we can be. When we walk with Christ and obey Him, our lives become a beautiful and bright spot in our mother's hearts. Christ is honored when we honor the women He chose to be our mothers.

Lord, may we always honor You

by honoring our mothers.

Thank You for choosing the

perfect mother for us. *Amen*

March 22

He Never Fails

"Do not fear, for I am with you;
do not be dismayed, for I am your God.
I will strengthen you and help you;
I will uphold you with My righteous right hand."
ISAIAH 41:10 NIV

James Hudson Taylor, of the China Inland Mission, wrote: "Depend on it. God's work done in God's way will never lack God's supply. He is too wise a God to frustrate His purposes for lack of funds, and He can just as easily supply them ahead of time as afterwards, and He much prefers doing so."

God always answers in the deeps, never in the shallows of our soul. The safest place to be is within the will of God. God's answers are wiser than our prayers.

Lord God, how we need to learn
to give everything to You.
May we recall easily that
You are able to do it all and that
You can be trusted. *Amen*

Forsake Sin

What have I to do anymore with idols?

HOSEA 14:8 NKJV

To "forsake" sin is *to leave it without any thought reserved of returning to it again.* Every time a man takes a journey from home about business we do not say he hath forsaken his house, because he meant, when he went out, to come to it again. No, but when we see a man leave his house, carry all his stuff away with him, lock up his doors, and take up his abode in another, never to dwell there more, here is a man hath indeed forsaken his house.

It were strange to find a drunkard so constant in the exercise of that sin, but some time you may find him sober, and yet a drunkard he is, as well as if he was then drunk … man forsakes his sin when he throws it from him, and bolts the door upon it with a purpose never to open more to it. Again observe, before pardon can be sealed he must "forsake," not this sin or that, but the whole "way."

~ William Gurnall

Lord, help us to throw our sin away,
never to return to it. *Amen*

March 24

Saints in the Making

Those also who suffer according to the will of God
shall entrust their souls to a faithful Creator
in doing what is right.

1 PETER 4:19

God did not promise us an easy life once we get saved. Actually, He tells us that we will have trials and tribulations. Some people seem to walk through their trials unscathed, while others struggle to accept that Christ is the one who is in control.

It is important to understand that culture, background and lifestyle all play a role in the way we react to trials. We are uniquely and wonderfully made, so it stands to reason that we will react to circumstances in our lives in uniquely different ways.

Father, help us to make room for You

to continue working in our lives

so that we will accept trials and pain,

recognizing that You are at work

on our behalf. *Amen*

March 25

The Good News

Believe in the Lord Jesus, and you will be saved,
you and your household.

ACTS 16:31

Statistics tell us that Christians win more souls to the Lord during the first two years after their conversion than in all the years from then until their death. The realization and joy over what Christ did for us soon takes a back seat to other things in our lives and we fail to tell the Good News to the lost around us.

The message of salvation remains the same ... Jesus came to earth to live and to shed His blood at Calvary as an atonement for our sins so that we could spend eternity with Him in heaven. How dare we withhold this, the Good News?

Jesus, You paid the ultimate

price for our salvation.

May we be eager to pass

the Gospel to those

around us. *Amen*

March 26

In His Presence

Come, let us worship and bow down,
let us kneel before the LORD our Maker.

PSALM 95:6

Let us go alone into His presence, for that is light, and fire, and life, and ceasing to be content with conventional religion let each one for himself and herself, in that awful Presence say, "O God, save me from mere correctness of view, and that curiosity to know, for the sake of knowing only, which has blighted my life, and make me what Thou wouldst have me to be in actual character."

~ G. Campbell Morgan

God, it takes time alone with You

for us to know how to believe.

Help us to not neglect time

in Your presence,

Holy Father. *Amen*

March 27

The Spirit of Love

Let us love one another, for love is of God.
1 JOHN 4:7 NKJV

For, as the Lamb of God, He has *all power* to bring forth in us a *sensibility* and a weariness of our own wrathful state, and a willingness to fall from it into meekness, humility, patience, and resignation to that mercy of God which alone can help us.

And when we are thus weary and heavy laden, and willing to get Rest to our Souls, in meek, humble, patient resignation to God, then it is, that He, as the *Light of God* and heaven, joyfully breaks in upon us, turns our darkness into light, our sorrow into joy, and begins that kingdom of God and divine love within us which will never have an end.

~ William Law

You tell us, God, to love others as You love us.
Help us to know You and love You
so that we will be able to love others. *Amen*

Sin Blocks Our View of Christ

*Our old self was crucified with Him,
in order that our body of sin
might be done away with,
so that we would no longer be slaves to sin.*

ROMANS 6:6

It's not enough to just know the content of the Bible — its stories, its sayings and its teachings. Unless you know the Author, the Bible is nothing more than just another book.

When you put your faith in Jesus Christ and have entered into a personal relationship with God the Father, the Bible truly becomes "living and active and sharper than any two-edged sword" (see Heb. 4:12).

Lord, help us to stand up for You

and not be the least bit intimidated.

We pray that this would be our goal.

Help us to be used by You to minister the Gospel

to a world that might know the words, but does not

know the person of Jesus Christ. *Amen*

March 29

God's Regard of Faith

Because of Christ and our faith in Him, we can now come boldly and confidently into God's presence.
EPHESIANS 3:12 NLT

A swallow having built its nest upon the tent of Charles V., the emperor generously commanded that the tent should not be taken down when the camp removed, but should remain until the young birds were ready to fly. Was there such gentleness in the heart of a soldier towards a poor bird which was not of his making, and shall the Lord deal hardly with His creatures when they venture to put their trust in Him!

Be assured He has a great love to those trembling souls that fly for shelter to His royal courts. He that builds his nest upon a divine promise shall find it abide and remain until he shall fly away to the land where promises are lost in fulfilments.

~ Charles H. Spurgeon

Father God, thank You for being faithful in Your promises. Please help me to trust You wholeheartedly. *Amen*

A Higher Calling

Godliness actually is a means of great gain.
1 TIMOTHY 6:6

A banker had no son to succeed him; however, his sister had married a man in poor circumstances and their only child was a bright boy. The banker visited the lad with an offer of an opportunity in his business, but he didn't reveal the purpose that is deep in his heart. The young man begins at the bottom, but as one position after another opens before him, he steps up to each in turn and fulfils his duties perfectly. He apprehends each part of his uncle's ideal as it is unveiled.

Years pass and one day the banker calls him into his office and offers the young man a partnership. This was what he intended from the start, but did not reveal his plan initially – he wanted his protégé to be prepared to use his opportunities and show his worth.

Lord, it is You who gives us worth.
Help us to take our responsibilities seriously,
knowing that You are concerned about
our higher calling in this world. *Amen*

March 31

Stand Firm!

Stand firm therefore,
having girded your loins with truth.
EPHESIANS 6:14 NKJV

The late Manley Beasley said, "The Christian experience begins with sitting and leads to walking, but it does not end with these. Every Christian must also learn to stand!"

It takes stamina to stand so the body must be prepared to stand for long periods of time. Sir Frances Drake spoke the following on the same subject: "Permanence, perseverance, and persistence in spite of all obstacles, discouragements, and impossibilities: It is this, that in all things distinguishes the strong soul from the weak." Timeless truths come from God's Word that will give us the strength we need to move forward for Christ while we labor in the kingdom of God here on earth.

Father, thank You for the encouragement
we find in the timeless truths that are available
to us every moment of every day. *Amen*

April

April 1

Steeped in Happiness

Blessed are the people who know the joyful sound!
They walk, O Lord, in the light of Your countenance.

PSALM 89:15 NKJV

The Bible speaks of God's joy and of laughter. We are supposed to be serious about certain things and there are times when laughter is out of place. However, God gave us smiles, laughter, happiness and the need to have some fun in our lives for a reason. Perhaps we should not squelch these wonderful emotions.

It is said that a smile can break the ice of the hardest heart. If that is so, think what full-blown laughter can do in a life that is filled with darkness and distress. Let's consider adding a bit of laughter to our lives so that "our joy might be full" (see John 15:11).

Father, help us to "go out with joy,
and be led forth with peace" (see Isa. 55:12)
that our souls shall be joyful. *Amen*

April 2

A Special Blessing

May the Lord cause you to increase and
abound in love for one another.

1 THESSALONIANS 3:12

Someone once wrote: "Mom, you've given me so much love from your heart and the warmth of your touch. You gave me the gift of life and you're a friend to me. We have a very special bond which only comes from God ... I'm sure you agree.

As a child I would say, 'Mommy, I love you.' Now you're my mother so dear and I love you even more with each new year. If I could have chosen, I would have picked no other ... than for you, to be my lifelong friend and precious mother."

Thank You, Lord, for the mothers

You have blessed us with.

Help us to never take them

for granted. *Amen*

A Birth Truth

*Now, brethren, I commend you to God
and to the Word of His grace,
which is able to build you up and
give you an inheritance among
all those who are sanctified.*
ACTS 20:32 NKJV

The believer who does not realize that he is eternally secure in Christ – a birth truth for babes – is certainly not going to be able to trust Him for emancipation from sin and maturity of growth.

Those who begin weakly, and are not instructed concerning their position in the Lord Jesus, are apt to remain weaklings. They move mainly up, down, and backward, with rarely any forward spiritual progress and abiding growth. For the most part, they subsist on experiences and so-called blessings; they seem to go from one crisis to another, never really settling down to reckon upon Christ risen as the source of their life here and now.

~ Miles J. Standford

Jesus, thank You, for our
eternal security. *Amen*

April 4

The Church

Let us not neglect our meeting together,
as some people do, but encourage one another.
HEBREWS 10:25 NLT

What is the church worth to a community? Such a question is like asking, "What is food worth to the body?" It is worth everything if it is worthy of its name. Down through the ages, the church has been the great power in the civilization of men and of nations.

The Christian church is and has always been the living exponent of decency and good government. It is the powerhouse of religion. It is the birthplace of more souls than any other place on earth. The church's one foundation is Jesus Christ the Lord.

Thank You, Lord,
for our churches. *Amen*

April 5

God Works in You

*It is God who works in you to will and to act
in order to fulfill His good purpose.*
PHILIPPIANS 2:13 NIV

It is God Himself dwelling in the heart of the believer. We are sometimes urged to "possess our possessions," but we would rather invite all true believers to possess their *possessor* – Jesus Christ Himself, "Who is all and in you all."

In fact, the word *imitate* really means "a going into." In this sense there is imitation indeed: for we enter into Christ, and Christ enters into us. So that we can say with Paul, "For me, to live is Christ" (Phil. 1:21); "Christ, who is our life" (Col. 3:4). We must remember that Christ *is* already in the heart of every believer. But unless He has *full* possession, and *full* control, we cannot have victory.

Thank You, Father,
for Your continuous
work in us. *Amen*

A Prayer for Peace

Lord, make me an instrument of Thy peace.

Where there is hatred, let me sow love;

Where there is injury, pardon;

Where there is doubt, faith;

Where there is despair, hope;

Where there is darkness, light;

Where there is sadness, joy.

O divine Master, grant that I may not so much seek

to be consoled as to console;

To be understood as to understand;

To be loved as to love;

For it is in giving that we receive;

It is in pardoning that we are pardoned;

It is in dying that we are born to eternal life.

~ St. Francis of Assisi

April 7

True Success

"Let your light shine before others, that they may see your good deeds and glorify your Father in heaven."
MATTHEW 5:16 NIV

To laugh often and much; to win the respect of intelligent people and the affection of children; to earn the appreciation of honest critics and endure the betrayal of false friends; to appreciate beauty; to find the best in others; to leave the world a bit better, whether by a healthy child, a garden patch or a redeemed social condition; to know even one life has breathed easier because you have lived. This is to have succeeded.

~ Ralph Waldo Emerson

Holy Spirit, please work in each of us
to do all we can to be all You want us to be
for Your kingdom here on earth. *Amen*

April 8

"It Is Finished!"

"It is finished!"
JOHN 19:30

Jesus has done all that the Holy Jehovah deemed necessary to be done to insure complete pardon, acceptance, and salvation to all who believe in His name. If you take Jesus as your Savior, you will build securely for eternity. "For no other foundation can anyone lay than that which is laid, which is Jesus Christ" (1 Cor. 3:11 NKJV).

He is the foundation-stone of salvation laid by God Himself, and on His finished atoning work alone you are instructed to rest the salvation of your soul, and not on anything accomplished by you, wrought in you, felt by you, or proceeding from you.

~ William Reed

Precious Jesus, how can we say "thank You"
except that we accept Your sacrifice and
come humbly before You. *Amen*

Time Together

*Let the husband render to his wife the affection due her,
and likewise also the wife to her husband.*

1 CORINTHIANS 7:3 NKJV

An elderly couple shared that the secret to their wonderful relationship: they loved God individually, and they loved God together. Every day of their married life, they would set aside some time to sit with a cup of coffee, tea, cheese and crackers, or even a glass of water, and just talk. They served each other and they talked about that day, their kids, their lives, Christ, and things that interested them.

They made a commitment that this special time was for positive conversation only: nothing negative or sad was to enter these private moments. They almost always ended up in each other's arms.

Father, thank You for loving

relationships and family.

Help us to cherish our loved ones.

We love You, Lord. *Amen*

April 10

The Sting of Death

"O Death, where is your sting?
O Hades, where is your victory?"
1 CORINTHIANS 15:55 NKJV

The day will dawn, when one of us shall harken in vain to hear a voice that has grown dumb, and morns will fade, noons pale, and shadows darken, while sad eyes watch for feet that never come.

One of us two must sometime face existence alone with memories that but sharpen pain and these sweet days shall shine back in the distance, like dreams of summer dawns, in nights of rain. One of us two, with tortured heart half broken, shall read long-treasured letters through salt tears, shall kiss with anguished lips each cherished token, that speaks of these love-crowned, delicious years. One of us two shall find all light, all beauty, all joy on earth, a tale forever done; shall know henceforth that life means only duty. Oh, God! Oh, God! Have pity on that one.

~ Ella Wilcox

God, You bore our grief. *Amen*

April 11

Freed from Troubles

The righteous has a refuge when he dies.

PROVERBS 14:32

A t death the saints shall be freed from all the troubles and encumbrances to which this life is subject. "Sin is the seed sown, and trouble is the harvest reaped." Life and trouble are married together. There is more in life to wean on than to tempt us.

Parents divide a portion of sorrow to their children, and yet leave enough for themselves. "Man is born to trouble;" he is heir to it, it is his birthright; you may as well separate weight from lead, as trouble from the life of man. … There are many things to embitter life and cause trouble, but death frees us from all. Blessed are the dead that die in the Lord; they rest from their labors.

~ Thomas Watson

For us who know You, Father,
death will be a wonderful, freeing rest.
Thank You for this gift. *Amen*

April 12

A Fine Art

[Love] always protects, always trusts,
always hopes, always perseveres.
1 CORINTHIANS 13:7 NIV

Men and women today are so caught up in the whirlwind of their busy lives that they have very little time to look up at the sky and nature around them, much less draw their spouse into the moment.

There is nothing, not a single thing, that should interfere with the loving relationship of a married couple. That is the only human relationship on earth God designed to come together at some point and remain intact until death. With something so important to the heart of God, it seems marriage could use some touching up to make it the fine art God intended it to be.

God, help us to love You as the head of marriage
and to love each other as one in marriage.
Bring love, touch, communication and laughter
back into the Christian marriage, we pray. *Amen*

April 13

Faith We Cannot See

We fix our eyes not on what is seen,
but on what is unseen,
since what is seen is temporary,
but what is unseen is eternal.

2 CORINTHIANS 4:18 NIV

Aiden Wilson Tozer once said, "Like the eye which sees everything in front of it and never sees itself, faith is occupied with the Object upon which it rests and pays no attention to itself at all. While we are looking at God, we do not see ourselves – blessed riddance.

The man who has struggled to purify himself and has had nothing but repeated failures will experience real relief when he stops tinkering with his soul and looks away to the perfect One."

Corrie ten Boom said, "Faith sees the invisible, believes the unbelievable and receives the impossible."

Father, help us to fix our eyes on You alone
and to have faith in Your Word. *Amen*

Love with the Love of God

Love does no harm to a neighbor;
therefore love is the fulfillment of the law.
ROMANS 13:10 NKJV

L ove may exist either as an affection or as an emotion. When love is an affection, it is voluntary, or consists in the act of the will. When it is an emotion, it is involuntary. What we call feelings, or emotions, are involuntary. They are not directly dependent on the will, or controlled by a direct act of will.

The virtue of love is mostly when it is in the form of an affection. The happiness of love is mostly when it is in the form of an emotion. If the affection of love be very strong, it produces a high degree of happiness, but the emotion of holy love is happiness itself.

~ Charles Finney

God, teach us, we pray, to love others
in the way You love us. *Amen*

Unique!

Your hands made me and fashioned me.
PSALM 119:73

God has created all that we know, all we see, and all that is to come. He has made each of us so uniquely different that right down to the properties of our blood, the DNA, no two of us are the same. No matter what gods people bow down to, they will never find a god who is able to do what our God alone can do.

An astronomer specialized in the study of snowflakes. Through a microscope, he photographed more than two thousand. Each snowflake was a geometrically perfect design and each one was unique. No two were identical. God, in manifesting His glory fashioned each snowflake from a new pattern. Is it conceivable that He would have no definite personal pattern for each of His children?

Father, You have done what no other
being can in making us unique.
Help us to recognize special traits in others
as we serve and love them. *Amen*

April 16

Early Will I Seek Thee

My heart is steadfast, O God,
my heart is steadfast.
PSALM 57:7

The intimacy of communion with Christ must be recaptured in the morning quiet time. Call it what you want — the quiet time, personal devotions, the morning watch, or individual worship — these holy minutes at the start of each day explain the inner secret of Christianity.

It's the golden thread that ties every great man of God together — from Moses to David Livingstone, the prophet Amos to Billy Graham — rich and poor, businessmen and military personnel. Every man who ever became somebody for God has this at the core of his priorities: time alone with God!

~ Robert D. Foster

May we desire to rise early and seek Your very heart

before we begin the tolls of the day before us.

Prepare us in this time, Father. *Amen*

Children of God

As many as received Him, to them He gave the right to become children of God, to those who believe in His name: who were born, not of blood, nor of the will of the flesh, nor of the will of man, but of God.

JOHN 1:12-13 NKJV

Jesus used the term "abba" (which means father or "daddy" in his Aramaic mother tongue) as an address in his prayers to God. There are no other examples of this usage in contemporary Judaism, but Jesus always addressed God in this way. The others perhaps regarded it as child's talk, a form of expression too disrespectful to be so used. But for Jesus, abba expressed the filial intimacy He felt toward His Father.

As the divine Son of the Father, Jesus enjoyed a unique relationship with Him, and His mission in the World consisted in opening up the blessings of sonship to those who believe.

~ Clark H. Pinnock

We pray, Lord, that we would be wise
sons and daughters, and that we would
come to know You as the intimate
and loving Father that You are. *Amen*

Every Perfect Gift

Every good thing given and
every perfect gift is from above.

JAMES 1:17

If there lurks in most modern minds the notion that to desire our goods and earnestly to hope for the enjoyment of it is a bad thing, I submit that this notion has crept in from Kant and the Stoics and is no part of the Christian faith.

Indeed, if we consider the unblushing promises of reward and the staggering nature of the rewards promised in the Gospels, it would seem that our Lord finds our desires not too strong, but too weak.

We are halfhearted creatures, fooling about with drink and sex and ambition when infinite joy is offered us, like an ignorant child who wants to go on making mud pies in a slum because he cannot imagine what is meant by the offer of a holiday at the sea. We are far too easily pleased.

We praise You, God, for all You do for us
and for the blessings You shower
down upon us each day. *Amen*

April 19

Share Your Bounty

*God is not unjust so as to forget your work and the love
which you have shown toward His name, in having
ministered and in still ministering to the saints.*
HEBREWS 6:10

How important it is for us to be hospitable. The Bible says, in Hebrews 13:2 to "not neglect to show hospitality to strangers, for by this some have entertained angels without knowing it."

Christians have such a wonderful opportunity to minister by opening their homes to friends, and their friends. There are so many hungry people all around us that could use a drink of water or a slice of bread. Most importantly, they probably need a friend, and perhaps a Savior. Let's not neglect the mission field just on the other side of our front door.

Lord, thank You for all You have blessed us with.

Help us, now, to share our bounty
with those in need. *Amen*

April 20

Divine Power

For the LORD is a great God and
a great King above all gods,
in whose hand are the depths of the earth.
PSALM 95:3-4

When God gives power, the only power He can give is divine power. God's own power! Not human power nor human ability! He did it in the past in Isaiah's day; He has done it since Isaiah's day, and as a matter of fact, even before Isaiah's day.

When the Jews had their backs to the wall, as it were, at the Red Sea and were facing certain annihilation, He gave power to the helpless, for Moses had said, "Stand still and see the deliverance of the Lord." You are helpless, you cannot fight, you cannot struggle, you cannot solve your problems. So stand aside and watch the Lord solve it.

~ R. B. Thieme

Lord God, it is You who has made everything
and who has everything under Your control.
Bless the name of Jesus. *Amen*

Our Provider

... I shall not want.
PSALM 23:1

Our Shepherd God provides for us – everything! We are so often concerned about food and housing that we overlook all the ways the Lord does provide. Psalm 23:1 says, "I shall not want," which implies, "I shall not want for anything" – materially, physically, emotionally or spiritually.

Our Shepherd does not only provide food and housing, but He also leads us to the right school, job, mate, church, and in all areas of our life. Everything we need in life is available through Him. He is our Counselor, High Priest, Provider, Purse Bearer. He hears our cries and is acquainted with our grief. He shelters us; He is our sufficiency!

Father God, thank You for being my all.
I pray that I will literally fall into Your arms,
allowing You to have complete control
of me and all that concerns me. *Amen*

April 22

Influencing the World

Prove yourselves to be blameless and innocent,
children of God above reproach in the midst
of a crooked and perverse generation,
among whom you appear as lights in the world.

PHILIPPIANS 2:15

We all influence! It's something we do many times each day ... we influence those around us. We have the capacity to influence for good and for bad, or evil. Even Christians sometimes influence in ways that don't represent Christ in a good way.

Being a good influence requires a lot of pruning, training, bending, willingness and obedience. When we get to that place of being so pliable in God's hands that He is our influence, then we can know that we are positioned to influence others in good and right ways – for His name's sake!

God, help us to be pliable in Your hands as You work Your perfect work in our lives. *Amen*

April 23

God's Tabernacle

"You are to be My holy people."

EXODUS 22:31 NIV

The Tabernacle is a picture of our redemption, and the grace of God. Since the Tabernacle follows the Ten Commandments, our sin and need of redemption is greatly emphasized. After looking hopelessly into the mirror of the law, we can turn and look with hope to God and His redemption.

Revealed in the Tabernacle we observe the divine holiness of God. Even this is more than we can truly understand. Even as a man died who broke the rules of the Tabernacle and touched something holy, so would we die except for the blood of Christ, which covers us, His children.

God, You are holy. We pray that as
You have made provision for Your children
to enter into a covenant relationship with You,
that our worship would honor You. *Amen*

April 24

Our Helper

"He will give you another Helper,
that He may be with you forever."
JOHN 14:16

Hope springs forth when we ask God to work in ways only He can. God calls each of us to a place of service and we are to pray for Him to work that call out in our lives. We continue to pray, never forgetting that it is God who ultimately does all the spiritual work, no matter how actively involved we are.

Without the work of the Holy Spirit, our labors are in vain. Perhaps that is the reason so many fail in the great commission. A call not covered in prayer is just that – a call! A call covered in prayer becomes the powerful working of the Holy Spirit.

Father, help us to pray for
the working of the Holy Spirit to be
actively at work in our lives. *Amen*

An Appointed Time

There is an appointed time for everything.

ECCLESIASTES 3:1

God is available and ready to pull the reins and get us headed in the right direction and in His appointed time. Sometimes it takes longer than at other times because we want a particular thing so desperately that we refuse to wait.

Those times come when we aren't spending time with Christ and trusting Him with our lives. Those are the times we take back our lives subconsciously, thinking we can handle things better than God. The timeless truth is that He does have a plan and a time to introduce it if we will learn from Him and trust Him with our whole being.

God, thank You for planning our
lives from the moment of birth
to the split second when we die –
and every moment in between.
Your love overwhelms us.
Thank You that our lives, for all time,
are appointed by You. *Amen*

Obey His Word

"Keep the commandments."
MATTHEW 19:17

We ought first to know that there are no good works except those which God has command-ed, even as there is no sin except that which God has forbidden. Therefore whoever wishes to know and to do good works needs nothing else than to know God's commandments …

Accordingly, we must learn how to distinguish among good works from the Commandments of God, and not from the appearance, the magnitude, or the number of the works themselves, nor from the judgment of men or of human law or custom, as we see has been done and still is done, because we are blind and despise the divine Commandments.

~ Martin Luther

Lord God, may the impact of the
Ten Commandments be at the forefront
of our hearts and minds
as we desire to obey You. *Amen*

April 27

Preparation Time

Our struggle is not against flesh and blood.
EPHESIANS 6:12

The Hebrews' experience of slavery shows how God used persecution to bless Himself, and His children. As persecution and seemingly impossible circumstances press in on us, we can always rely on God's presence. Baby Moses' miraculous preservation is a wonderful example of God's guiding hand. When utterly helpless, God remains absolute and constant.

The years that Moses was in preparation compared to his actual time of service are evidence of the importance of preparation. The biggest time of preparation in the life of a Christian is that time spent with God – alone. If we meet God on the mountain, the fighting in the valley is much easier. Much time must be spent before God for even a short time of service.

God, help us to know You in times of persecution, preparation, and when we recognize Your presence. *Amen*

April 28

Looking Upward

The LORD will accomplish what concerns me.
PSALM 138:8

The story goes that the sea looked toward heaven, gazing upon the beauty of the puffy white clouds and wanted to be a cloud. The sea worked very hard until it tossed itself up into the air, only to fall back upon a rock. It was of no use; the sea could not be a cloud.

The sun, watching the struggle below, said to the sea, "Be quiet, be still, and just look at me." The sea obeyed and was quiet and stopped struggling. The sun began to shine brighter and brighter and the sea felt its moisture moving upward until suddenly, next to the puffy white cloud, appeared a second cloud. What the sea could not do, no matter how hard he tried, the sun was able to do simply because the sea looked to it.

Lord, help us to look to
You and trust! *Amen*

April 29

Shut in, Not Out

"If you ask Me anything in My name, I will do it."
JOHN 14:14

A dear saint, a shut-in caused by a physical ailment, committed to praying. He called upon the omnipotent Christ to perform His amazing miracles in the lives of those he knew, as well as those he only saw moving outside his window but never met.

Though he couldn't touch those he prayed for; he was able to ask God, and to trust Him, to touch them. He saw God move mountains in the lives of those he prayed for. He left an eternal legacy that will continue for generations because He did not give up, but allowed God to use him in his infirmities to minister to others.

God, please make us see that
every circumstance in life is an
opportunity to minister to this world.
Help us to use every moment to
bless You. *Amen*

April 30

In His Strength

All things to work together for good
to those who love God.
ROMANS 8:28 NKJV

We must daily see God's grace-sufficiency. Many times in the existence of self-sufficiency, God has to make unusable or inoperative our own self to make room for Him to work. He has to show us how much we need Him, how small we are on our own.

We have to go through times of trouble and endure pain in order to recognize the real Source of our strength. We waste much time; all of the time we spend in our own strength, all of the time we spend depending upon the natural is wasted time, in a sense. We struggle to accomplish something when all we have to do is turn to God, who is always ready to work out everything in the best way possible.

Father, show us, through Your Word,
how to rely on Your strength,
and to use our time wisely. *Amen*

May

Iron Bars

"I will give you rest."
MATTHEW 11:28

Richard Lovelace wrote *To Althea, from Prison* while serving for royalist sympathies. He understood that many inmates, though surrounded by bars, are not in prison; they are free – internally. He also understood that many are without the iron bars, but are under such bondage that bars of hopelessness surround them. Most of us experience a time when the pressure is so great that we feel being behind prison walls would be a better place to be.

That feeling of imprisonment, no matter how great the trial, will pass and we can move away from that time, whereas the prisoner must continue to endure the bars that do surround them. "Stone walls do not a prison make, nor iron bars a cage!"

Lord, we pray for Your peaceful
rest to enter the hearts of
prisoners of any kind. *Amen*

May 2

Thy Will Be Done

If we ask anything according to His will,
He hears us.
1 JOHN 5:14 NKJV

Let us have a great esteem of the Lord's prayer; let it be the model and pattern of all our prayers. There is a double benefit arising from framing our petitions suitably to this prayer. Hereby error in prayer is prevented.

It is not easy to write wrong after this copy; we cannot easily err when we have our pattern before us. Hereby mercies requested are obtained; for the apostle assures us that God will hear us when we pray "according to His will." And sure we pray according to His will when we pray according to the pattern He has set us. So much for the introduction to the Lord's prayer, "After this manner pray ye."

~ Thomas Watson

May we always pray
according to Your will,
Holy God. *Amen*

Doubt

"If you have faith,
and do not doubt ... it will happen."
MATTHEW 21:21

Doubts visit the Christian daily. Because of this overwhelming emotion, we must know who we are in Christ. We must know Him and, yes, we must know who Satan is so we can recognize his work.

Peter was oblivious to the huge waves that surrounded him as he heard the Lord tell him to step out of the boat and walk on the water. Once he began to doubt, he saw – instantly – all the dangers around him as he took his eyes off Christ. Doubt caused him to sink. Doubt will do the same thing to ... cause us to sink. Keeping our eyes on Jesus through faith is what we need to do so we can make it to every shore in life.

Help us, Lord, to have faith
that is dead to doubts,
dumb to discouragements,
and blind to impossibilities. *Amen*

Follow the Leader

"He goes before them;
and the sheep follow him,
for they know his voice."
JOHN 10:4 NJKV

Former President Eisenhower used to explain leadership by laying a string on a table and pulling it. As he pulled it, the string always followed. Then he would stop and push the string and it would lay motionless until he pulled it again. He said, "Pull the string, and it will follow wherever you wish. Push it, and it will go nowhere at all."

A good leader sets the example by leading and not by pushing. As Christians, we often fail to follow Christ's leadership. It is our choice to follow God or we may find ourselves being pushed right out of His blessings.

Lord, You lead in paths of righteousness.
Help us to always follow You. *Amen*

Grace in Forgiveness

"Forgive us our debts."
MATTHEW 6:12

A shamefaced employee was summoned to the office of the senior partner to hear his doom. The least that he could expect was a blistering dismissal: he might be sent to prison for years. The old man called his name and asked him if he were guilty. The clerk stammered that he had no defense. "I shall not send you to prison," said the old man. "If I take you back, can I trust you?"

When the surprised and broken clerk had given assurance and was about to leave, the senior partner continued: "You are the second man who has fallen and been pardoned in this business. I was the first. What you have done, I did. The mercy you have received, I received. It is only the grace of God that can keep us both."

Father, help us to practice
forgiveness in our
daily living. *Amen*

May 6

Welcome Home

You were formerly darkness,
but now you are Light in the Lord.
EPHESIANS 5:8

Tony Orlando and Dawn, a popular singing trio of the Eighties, became famous for their song titled *Tie a Yellow Ribbon Round the Old Oak Tree*. When the Gulf War broke out in the early Nineties, America adopted that song and we saw huge yellow ribbons hanging all over neighborhoods and in store fronts from the East coast to the West, and regions beyond.

Imagine the prodigal son returning home after misappropriating his inherence and having to survive by eating swine's food. He must have seen the colors of a joyful welcome when his father prepared a feast fit for a king on his return.

Father, we are all prodigals
at some time in our lives.
I pray that we would always
know Your arms of welcome. *Amen*

May 7

Hope!

To them God willed to make known
what are the riches of the glory
of this mystery among the Gentiles:
which is Christ in you, the hope of glory.
COLOSSIANS 1:27 NKJV

Martin Luther said, "Everything that is done in the world is done by hope." This is so true! Think about it – we do hope in everything. We hope for a good day, time with our families, a good job with timely pay increases, and we hope for the best in everything.

Some people also hope for things that aren't necessary or even good for them. We hope for good and bad. What are *you* hoping for in life? In eternity? Is your hope securely focused on a Holy God? Or are you looking to manmade gods – idols? God is able to control everything relating to humankind and all that influences our decisions. We must yield under the mighty hand of God so that our hope is directed toward Him.

Father, help our hearts to turn toward You in faith, and dependence, and hope. *Amen*

In the Beginning

The battle is the LORD's.
1 SAMUEL 17:47 NKJV

God so wants us to understand that a conflict exists between Satan and Christ. Since the Garden of Eden, it has been raging full-blast in every age and circumstance. This is the basis for all war and conflict that have occurred, and that will occur in the future.

Of even more importance is the fact that this is the basis of all of our struggles and troubles in everyday life. Satan constantly attempts to corrupt us and to destroy our fellowship with God, but God is always there, able and ready to purify us. God pursues and pleads with us, even when we turn our back on Him and go our own way. He continually offers Himself in His mercy and justice.

God, we desperately need You
to help us recognize the enemy
and to move to victory in You. *Amen*

May 9

Supernatural Power

The LORD blessed him.
JUDGES 13:24

Supernaturally, Samson did more physically than all of the naturally strong men in that day. He knew the Lord was his strength. God can do with us whatever He likes. He is not hindered if we belong fully to Him. Our strength leaves us at the first sign of sin. Sin hinders God's power in our lives and we, too, can be bound by Satan as a prisoner. Power and strength come from separation unto the Lord, not separation from the world. Separation from the world without separation unto God leaves a dry, dead life.

When Samson turned from God, he lost everything he had. All left him, but the Lord accepted him when he came back in repentance. He had a secret! The Lord was his strength. The Spirit gave him supernatural power.

We look to You, Lord,
for our strength. *Amen*

The Glory of the Impossible

"With God all things are possible."
MATTHEW 19:26

There was never a truer word than this: "The revelation of my growth in grace is the way I look on obedience" (Oswald Chambers). The call to do the impossible may seem to be the counsel of despair, but as we become accustomed to habitual obedience, such calls come with delight. They inspire us with new zest and new zeal. Such has been called "the glory of the impossible."

George Müller learned this rare lesson in the school of faith and obedience. As he faced a new Red Sea of impossibilities, he said, "I had a secret satisfaction in the greatness of the difficulties which were in the way. So far from being cast down on account of them they delighted my soul; for I desired only to do the will of the Lord in the matter."

Thank You, Lord, for grace that
turns impossibilities
into possibilities. *Amen*

Consecrated to God

The LORD said, "Surely I will be with you."
JUDGES 6:16

The closer to the Lord, the more severe Satan's attacks can be, as was the case of Gideon. Much preparation is required by God for Him to move us to the place of His choosing. As we move in relationship toward God, He can bless us with more power to fight off the foe and to work for Him. Satan can use anyone, for all of us can fall into his clutches.

We must continually draw near to God for deliverance and safety. The Lord is our Guide, and He has the answers we need. His way is clear and perfect. God wants disciples, not halfhearted followers. He does more when He has full control of a few than when He has partial control of many.

Lord, we consecrate ourselves to You
to use for Your work here on earth. *Amen*

Victory in Christ

*Yours, O LORD, is the greatness and the power
and the glory and the victory and the majesty.*
1 CHRONICLES 29:11

Unmovable walls. Just as the enormous walls of Jericho lay between Israel and conquest, so many impossible problems lie between us and conquest of what Christ desires for us. Unmovable walls moved. It couldn't happen, but it did. And it happened, not "by force or by might."

There was no human answer, and today there is no answer within us for victory. As Christ responded to faith, expressed in obedience at Jericho, so He does today. He is our victory. The two conditions of victory are surrender of all to God and faith in Him to deliver us from all sin into full victory. He has the answer to every problem.

Lord, "let all our strength be hurled,
faith is the victory that overcomes
the world" (John H. Yates). *Amen*

May 13

Used for Good

By faith Rahab the harlot did not perish.
HEBREWS 11:31

She was probably one of the most wicked women in all of Jericho. She was likely one of the lowest women concerning morality of her time. She was, however, transformed by God. Then she risked her own life to save two of God's servants, and cooperated in every way to fulfill God's purposes. She and her house were spared from sure destruction.

Most of us have felt that God would never forgive something we did and that He would never be able to use us for good. God takes lives, no matter where they have been, and transforms them. Then, He uses them for good.

God, we all have a past, some pretty awful.

You are a God of futures and

we pray that You would take

us out of the pit and transform us

through Your glorious light. *Amen*

May 14

Mother's Day

*Can a woman forget her nursing child and
have no compassion on the son of her womb?
Even these may forget, but I will not forget you.*
ISAIAH 49:15

Contemporary critics of our swift-moving time are accustomed to feel or express deep sorrow over the passing of "the home" as other generations knew it. There is much of a challenge in such contemplation. Civilization is built on "the home" – for which neither school, nor church, nor state can substitute.

The same old Mother-love, at most family shrines, is constant as the hills. Where it is not, this day has a maternal challenge quite as much as a challenge to the younger folk – because the tragedy of tragedies is to fail to earn the blessed obeisance which this day admonishes throughout the year.

Father, thank You for the gift of mothers.
Help us to always honor them. *Amen*

May 15

Our Heavenly Teacher

Give attention to my words.
PROVERBS 4:20

Board certified, with credentials to teach us anything He wants us to know, Christ knows the truth. He is truth. He teaches all day, every day, for life; His classroom is the world. He promised tests of trials and tribulations. Pop quizzes come on a regular basis — they can be short and take only a few minutes, or they can last a long time! The topic: God's Will for Your Life 101!

Good teachers know their students. God knew us in our mother's womb; He knows the hairs on our head; He speaks our native tongue — nationality and location are not barriers for Him. He knows the content of each lesson, He knows us by name, and He has the means to teach us the lessons He has for us. Our responsibility should then be to stand back and get ready for the greatest lesson of all.

Jesus, teach us, we pray,
and also make us teachable. *Amen*

Justification and Wisdom

God is the one who justifies.

ROMANS 8:33

A full pardon: that is what God can do for you. Not because you are innocent, for "all have sinned" and are guilty, but because Jesus Christ bore the penalty of your guilt in His body on the cross. He died in your stead, took your place, and now, since your sin, all of it, has been imputed to Him, God can justify you, and account you righteous. He can pronounce you "not guilty." Justification is the judicial act of God whereby He declares righteous one who believes in Christ.

The prophet Micah instructs us, "Do justly, love mercy, and walk humbly with your God" (6:8).

God, we pray that we would seek justice,

Your justice in our courts today.

We pray that never an innocent one

would be placed behind bars for

a crime they did not commit.

We pray for Your wisdom. *Amen*

Bring Ye All the Tithes

*"Bring the whole tithe into the storehouse,
so that there may be food in My house,
and test Me now in this," says the LORD of hosts,
"if I will not open for you the windows of heaven
and pour out for you a blessing until it overflows."*

MALACHI 3:10

College students struggle to survive as it is, but to give up a tithe, though only one tenth of their earnings, creates an even greater struggle. God really doesn't need the money, right?

However, once a person commits to giving the small amount Christ says is to go into the storehouse, He also says He will bless in abundance the nine tenths left. Many can testify to the way God has blessed them when they tithe. Tithing is not an option for the Christian, it is a blessing.

Father, help us to give to You
what is already Yours. *Amen*

May 18

Take Time to Be Holy

*Let the word of Christ dwell in you
richly in all wisdom.*
COLOSSIANS 3:16 NKJV

There is no time so profitably spent as the early hour given to Jesus only. Do we give sufficient attention to this hour? If possible, it should be redeemed; nothing can make up for it. We must take time to be holy!

One other thought. When we bring our questions to God, do we not sometimes either go on to offer some other petition, or leave the closet without waiting for replies? Does not this seem to show little expectation of an answer, and little desire for one? Should we like to be treated so? Quiet waiting before God would save from many a mistake and from many a sorrow.

~ J. Hudson Taylor

Father, we need to know You

so that we can serve You more faithfully.

Help us to desire to be with You, in Your Word,

so it will dwell richly in us in all wisdom. *Amen*

May 19

Genuine Worship

Worship the LORD.
PSALM 2:11

Worship is the highest expression of that for which we were created. In true worship, God is all that matters. True worship is spiritual – we are in the Spirit. The Holy Spirit in us is to be the life of the glorified Jesus.

Dean Sherman said, "The reason we exist is not just to have big, happy churches. We are to live and worship and proclaim the Word of God to the nations and peoples of the earth. This will drive back the powers of darkness and implement every intention of the heart of God."

God, we worship You, we adore You,
and we honor You. *Amen*

A Supernatural Cure

God is faithful, who will not allow you to be tempted
beyond what you are able,
but with the temptation will provide
the way of escape also.

1 CORINTHIANS 10:13

In biblical times, there was no natural cure for leprosy. Today, and such will forever be the case, a natural cure for sin is unknown. Christ, however, is the supernatural cure for both. All the problems of leprosy were cured by God. All of the problems sin brings have been cured by Christ on the cross. We must recognize that we are sinners, confess our sins, repent of them, and ask Christ to be our Lord and Savior.

God's Word says that God is faithful and just to forgive our sins (see 1 John 1:9). He wants us to come to Him in childlike faith and trust what He has already done for us. When Christ hung on the cross and said, "It is finished," the victory was won for all who accept Him.

As we look at sin, help us to know
the victory that is ours in You, Jesus. *Amen*

May 21

Necessary Pruning

The fruit of the righteous is a tree of life.
PROVERBS 11:30

The wait is worth it when fruit trees bear an abundance of luscious, plump fruit. Farmers know this means a yield that will bring in a hefty income and grocers are able to sell more when the presentation is appealing. Customers will return to purchase more of what they enjoyed the first time when the taste is good. Moms love serving their families healthy fruit that is also flavorful.

It is no easy task growing quality fruit. The vine or tree requires tending and cultivating while considering all the elements that could potentially destroy it. The Bible tells us that we, God's children, are branches that also require tending by the true vinedresser, who is God. He will nourish us and help us to grow to be mighty men and women in Christ if we will submit to the necessary pruning.

God, may we bear fruit for You. *Amen*

The Heart of Mercy

When we are judged, we are disciplined by the Lord so that we will not be condemned along with the world.

1 CORINTHIANS 11:32

Some of our confessed sin results in punishment. When suffering for our sins, we can trust God to do what is best and just for us and for all involved. God's punishment for sin shows His hatred for sin.

After we sin, God does something and He expects us to do something. He works in our hearts to convict us of our sin, and we are to confess and repent. He holds us accountable and we are to take responsibility. The pearl of justice is found in the heart of mercy.

~ St. Catherine of Sinea

God, You are a God of justice.

Help us to love Your ways,

which are pure and right. *Amen*

May 23

I Can't See a Thing!

We walk by faith, not by sight.
2 CORINTHIANS 5:7

We fret about not seeing any growth in our lives as Christians. We try "this and that" and still all appears as before. God says if we are in His will (by surrender and faith) we *are* growing. When Elisha saw the seed fall in the ground and die, something was still growing – inside him – and it was faith!

So often we are so harsh on ourselves that we actually interrupt the growth process. God is always at work in the lives of Christians. The Lord wants us to walk by faith, because our eyes can be deceived: And even though our path may fade, God's Word can always be believed.

We pray, Lord, and trust the living Word
of God in faith to embrace Your timeless truths.
Amen

The Best Lesson

Train up a child in the way he should go,
even when he is old he will not depart from it.

PROVERBS 22:6

The best lesson that a child can learn at home, that a pupil can learn at school, or that a collegian can learn at college is the lesson of obedience, respect for constituted authority. It counts for more in the building up of character than acquaintance with the spelling book or familiarity with the classics, the sciences or the philosophies.

The spirit obedience is the material of character, and character is capital, while scholarship is only an implement to be put at the service of capital. Life is constantly testing you.

Holy Spirit, we pray that You would help us
to recall the lessons learned from our parents
as they taught us from Your Word.
Help us to obey the truth. *Amen*

May 25

Prayers Answered

The effective prayer of a righteous
man can accomplish much.
JAMES 5:16

Yea, however weak our faith may be, God will try it; only with this restriction, that as in every way, He leads on gently, gradually, patiently, so also with reference to the trial of our faith. At first our faith will be tried very little in comparison with that it may be afterwards: for God never lays more upon us that He is willing to enable us to bear.

Now when the trial of faith comes, we are naturally inclined to distrust God, and to trust ourselves, or our friends, or in circumstances. Would the believer, therefore, have his faith strengthened, he must especially, give time to God.

~ George Müller

Father, as we put our trust in You in faith,

please continue to lead us on gently,

gradually and patiently. *Amen*

Thorough Cleansing

Draw near to God and He will draw near to you.
Cleanse your hands, you sinners;
and purify your hearts, you double-minded.

JAMES 4:8

A college freshman went to the dorm laundry room with his dirty clothes bundled into an old sweatshirt. But he was so embarrassed by how dirty his clothes were that he never opened the bundle. He merely pushed it into a washer and dryer and finally took the still-unopened bundle back to his room.

He discovered, of course, that the clothes had gotten wet and then dry, but not clean. God says, "Don't keep your sins in a safe little bundle. I want to do a thorough cleansing in your life – all the dirty laundry of your life."

Jesus, You have given us every possible

opportunity to come to You for cleansing.

Help us not to hide the dirt of our lives from You.

Help us to come for a complete cleansing. *Amen*

May 27

Contented Living

The steps of a good man are ordered by the LORD,
and He delights in his way.

PSALM 37:23 NKJV

Cast not away your confidence because God defers His performances. That which does not come in your time, will be hastened in His time, which is always the more convenient season.

God will work when He pleases, how He pleases, and by what means He pleases. He is not bound to keep our time, but He will perform His word, honor our faith, and reward them that diligently seek Him.

~ Matthew Henry

May we allow You, Father,

to order our steps so that

we may walk out the plan You

have for our lives. *Amen*

May 28

Heavenly Mansions

"I go to prepare a place for you."

JOHN 14:2

How amazing that God loved us so much that He gave His only Son so that we could have life eternal. He loves us so much that He is preparing a home for us ... a mansion, no less. This is not like any mansion we have here on earth. It is not a manmade one, but a dwelling place that God is designing just for you and for me.

There isn't a home building or decoration show that could come up with a plan like the one God has for us. The Master Builder is working out the details for us right now. This is such an incredibly glorious thought that it overwhelms us to imagine what God is doing for us. Hallelujah!

Father, we look forward to
seeing You in heaven.
Until that glorious day,
lead us in the paths of
righteousness. *Amen*

Wisdom from Above

If any of you lacks wisdom, let him ask of God,
who gives to all liberally.

JAMES 1:5 NKJV

I called upon God, and the Spirit of Wisdom came to me. I preferred her before scepters and thrones, and esteemed riches as nothing in comparison to her. Neither compared I unto her any precious stone, because all gold, in respect of her, is as a little sand; and silver shall be counted as clay to her.

I loved her above health and beauty, and chose to have her instead of light; for the light that cometh from her never goeth out. All good things together came to me with her, and innumerable riches in her hands. And I rejoiced in them all, because Wisdom goeth before them.

~ The Wisdom of Solomon, Apocrypha

Lord, it is the desire of our heart
to have wisdom so that we would make
decisions that can be blessed by You. *Amen*

May 30

Christ with Us

He delivered me from my strong enemy, from those who hated me, for they were too strong for me. They confronted me in the day of my calamity, but the LORD was my support. He also brought me out into a broad place; He delivered me because He delighted in me.

PSALM 18:17-19 NKJV

That's life! If we face our problems and respond to them positively, and refuse to give in to panic, bitterness, or self-pity ... the adversities that come along to bury us usually have within them the potential to benefit and bless us!

Remember that forgiveness, faith, prayer, praise and hope ... all are excellent ways to "shake it off and step up" out of the wells in which we find ourselves!

Father, help us not to forget

to call upon Your name,

for You know the adversity

we face daily as well as the adversary.

Thank You, Lord. *Amen*

May 31

Encourage One Another

When you walk, their counsel will lead you.
When you sleep, they will protect you.
When you wake up, they will advise you.
PROVERBS 6:22 NLT

Encouraging others with scriptural affirmations is a powerful way to help someone who is struggling for whatever reason. A simple note with a verse that helps to build up a friend could be the very thing they need to overcome the difficulty they are dealing with.

A card to a friend who may seem to be doing well will bless and encourage them by letting them know you are thinking of them. God, in His wisdom, made us to be people who know how to encourage. How wonderful it would be if we took more time to do what we are actually very good at.

Lord, as we seek to reach out to those around us with encouragement, we pray that discouraging thoughts and words would depart from us. *Amen*

June

June 1

God's Representatives

Your life will be brighter than the noonday.
Even darkness will be as bright as morning.
JOB 11:17 NLT

Standing for what you believe in, regardless of the odds against you, and the pressure that tears at your resistance – means courage. Keeping a smile on your face, when inside you feel like dying, for the sake of supporting others – means strength. Stopping at nothing, and doing what's in your heart, you know is right – means determination. Doing more than is expected, to make another's life a little more bearable, without uttering a single complaint – means compassion.

Helping a friend in need, no matter the time or effort, to the best of your ability – means loyalty. Giving more than you have, and expecting nothing in return – means selflessness. Holding your head high facing each difficulty with the confidence that time will bring you better tomorrows, and never giving up – means confidence.

Jesus, we are Your representatives. Help us to reflect Your love and light to the world. *Amen*

The Burden Bearer

God did this so that they would seek Him
and perhaps reach out for Him and find Him,
though He is not far from any one of us.

ACTS 17:27 NIV

Phillips Brooks said, The little sharp vexations and the briars that cut the feet, why not take all to the Helper who has never failed us yet? Tell Him about the heartache, and tell Him the longings too, tell Him the baffled purpose when we scarce know what to do. Then, leaving all our weakness with the One divinely strong. Forget that we bore the burden and carry away the song.

Someone once wrote, "Remember the tea kettle: though up to its neck in hot water, it continues to sing."

Lord Jesus Christ, we need to be mindful of the things that would trip us up and intimidate us. Lord, when the enemy is trying to gain a stronghold, help us to sing above the confusion. *Amen*

Golden Opportunities

*Your ears will hear a word behind you,
"This is the way, walk in it,"
whenever you turn to the right or to the left.*

ISAIAH 30:21

Famous United States statesman, diplomat, inventor and printer, Benjamin Franklin, was also a practical man. He once said that, "To succeed, jump as quickly at opportunities as you do at conclusions."

He would have agreed with Sir Winston Churchill's concept about opportunity: "A pessimist sees the difficulty in every opportunity; an optimist sees the opportunity in every difficulty." God has unlimited opportunities for the one who comes to Him and seeks the perfect place to serve Him. Whether on the home front or abroad, the list is endless.

Lord God, help us to recognize when Your opportunities come and be prepared in advance to take up the challenge and do the work at hand. *Amen*

Wisdom, Knowledge and Joy

God gives wisdom and knowledge and joy to a man who is good in His sight.
ECCLESIASTES 2:26 NKJV

What are the important things in your life? Time with your loved ones? Your faith? Your education, dreams, a worthy cause, teaching, mentoring?

Remember to find room for them before the other smaller things, or you'll never get them into your life at all. Prioritize your life and God will give you wisdom, knowledge and joy.

"Behold, You desire truth in the innermost being, and in the hidden part You will make me know wisdom. (Psalm 51:6)."

God of all knowledge and wisdom,
help us to pay attention and ensure we make
time for the truly important things in life. *Amen*

Everyday Wonders

I will tell of all Your marvelous works.
PSALM 9:1-2 NKJV

When students were asked to list what they thought were the present Seven Wonders of the World, the teacher noted that one quiet student hadn't turned in her paper. She asked the girl if she was having trouble with her list. The girl replied, "Yes, a little. I couldn't quite make up my mind, because there were so many." The teacher replied, "Well, tell us what you have, and maybe we can help."

The girl hesitated, then read, "I think the Seven Wonders of the World are: to see, to taste, to touch, to hear, to feel, to laugh, or smile, and most of all ... to love. The room was so silent you could have heard a pin drop. Those things we overlook as simple and "ordinary" are truly wondrous.

Thank You, God for all the wondrous and majestic things You have done for us. *Amen*

June 6

Understanding Loss

Even though our outward man is perishing,
yet the inward man is being renewed day by day.
2 CORINTHIANS 4:16 NKJV

We all experience loss — loss of people, loss of jobs, loss of relationships, loss of independence, loss of steam, loss of things.

When what you held dear can be viewed as a gift, a wonder that you had it at all, the memory can eventually become one more of gratitude than tragedy. And you will discover the healing you need.

"My flesh and my heart may fail, but God is the strength of my heart and my portion forever" (Psalm 73:26).

Holy God, loss is so difficult for us,
but we know that You have
not forsaken us in our hour of grief.
We pray for Your comfort as You, Lord,
hold us in Your arms. *Amen*

June 7

Wash Us and Cleanse Us

Wash me thoroughly from my iniquity and cleanse me from my sin. For I know my transgressions, and my sin is ever before me. Against You, You only, I have sinned and done what is evil in Your sight, so that You are justified when You speak and blameless when You judge.

PSALM 51:2-4

The Bible says that if we open our hearts to the Spirit of God, He will fill us with a holy hatred of sin, and with the hunger and thirst of a new life. If we act upon the suggestion, we will be delivered from our sins that defile our whole lives. All that the Bible says in this respect is true.

God, wash our sins away by the blood of Your Son and help us to live new lives that are committed to You. *Amen*

Come to Him

The LORD is with you while you are with Him.
If you seek Him, He will be found by you;
but if you forsake Him, He will forsake you.
2 CHRONICLES 15:2 NKJV

Walking through the city slums, an atheistic barber asked the preacher: "This is why I cannot believe in a God of love. If God was as kind as you say, He would not permit all this poverty, disease, and squalor. He would not allow these poor bums to be addicted to dope and other character-destroying habits." They met a man who was especially dirty, hair hanging down his neck, with a half-inch of stubble on his face. Said the minister: "You can't be a very good barber or you wouldn't permit a man like that to continue living in this neighborhood without a haircut and shave."

Indignantly the barber answered: "Why blame me for that man's condition? I can't help it that he is like that. He has never come in my shop: I could fix him up and make him look like a gentleman!" The minister said: "Then don't blame God for allowing the people to continue in their evil ways, when He is constantly inviting them to come and be saved."

Lord, help us to seek You.

June 9

Not Ashamed

Those who trust in themselves are fools,
but those who walk in wisdom are kept safe.
PROVERBS 28:26 NIV

Many have attempted to prove that God does not exist, but none have ever succeeded and many have actually met the Lord in their efforts to prove their theories. Christians have platforms offered to them almost daily to proclaim truth, but we often refuse to take advantage of them. Each missed opportunity could be the difference between life and death for that one we turned away from.

When called upon to testify about your faith in Christ, ask God to help you to be prepared to share your salvation experience and your faith in Christ Jesus, and not turn away. God will give you the power and the words so that His message will be proclaimed when we yield to Him.

Lord, may we be active in proclaiming
the Gospel message and not ashamed
to share our faith in You. *Amen*

June 10

A Godly Woman

*She is clothed with strength and dignity,
and she laughs without fear of the future.
When she speaks, her words are wise, and she gives
instructions with kindness. She carefully watches
everything in her household and suffers nothing from
laziness. Her children stand and bless her. Her husband
praises her: "There are many virtuous and capable
women in the world, but you surpass them all!"*

PROVERBS 31:25-29 NLT

A virtuous woman is one who possesses moral character; she is above reproach, she is excellent in general and she is respected. The woman in Proverbs 31 is an example of a godly woman. The attributes she possesses are those that all women should strive for.

Father, may Christian women today
seek to be a Proverbs 31 woman.
Help them to stand strong against the
pressures and allure of this world. *Amen*

Begin with Worship

*"You shall worship the LORD your God,
and Him only you shall serve."*
MATTHEW 4:10 NKJV

The pastor of a large church in South Korea is a man who has spent much of his life on his knees. He rises every morning and prays for two to three hours. This pastor is a humble man, a powerful minister of the gospel, and one whom God has blessed in his family and his ministry. He is respected and revered not only in Korea, but around the world.

When in conversation with him, it is obvious that he knows well the One he talks about because each day he bows before God to worship and learn from Him. The best way to begin the day is on our knees in worship to God who gives us the day.

God, we pray that our worship will bless You,
for You are worthy of our praise.
Help us to start each day with You. *Amen*

June 12

Humbly Pray

*"If My people who are called by My name
will humble themselves, and pray and seek My face,
and turn from their wicked ways, then I will hear from
heaven, and will forgive their sin and heal their land."*
2 CHRONICLES 7:14 NKJV

Yea the God who holds the sea in the hollow of His
hand; the God who swings this ponderous globe
of earth in its orbit more easily than you could swing
a child's toy rubber ball; the God who marshals the
stars and guides the planets in their blazing paths with
undeviating accuracy; the God of Sinai, and of Horeb;
the heaven-creating, devil-conquering, dead-raising
God – it is the very God who says to you and to me: "If
ye ask, I will do!"

~ James McConkey

Lord God, help us to draw
near to You, to listen to You,
and to learn from You. *Amen*

June 13

Mother, Read to Me

My mouth is filled with Your praise and
with Your glory all day long.
PSALM 71:8

When a mother reads to her children, a hush comes over the whole room. Children can learn more from books than just about any other way. When a mother begins reading to her children while in the womb and continues that practice for as long as she can, the child develops a desire to read.

When a mother reads the Bible to her children, their desire will be turned toward Christ. What a wonderful thing for a mother to hear the adult she read to as a child praising God all day long.

Jesus, thank You for Your Word
that we can read to our children,
giving them a reason to praise
You all day long. *Amen*

June 14

Sweet Communion with Christ

I will praise You with music on the harp, because You are faithful to Your promises, O my God. I will sing praises to You with a lyre, O Holy One of Israel.

PSALM 71:22 NLT

Christ desires that we experience sweet times of communion fellowship with Him. It does not matter if everything around us appears to be nothing but gloom.

Just take a moment and listen; listen to what God has for us as we enjoy the sweetest of His music in your hearts. He so graciously warms us with His tenderness when we need it most.

We praise You, God, for times of sweet communion with You, even in the midst of painful circumstances. You are constant and we thank You, Lord, for the comfort You bring to us. *Amen*

June 15

The Joy of the Lord

In Your presence is fullness of joy;
in Your right hand there are pleasures forever.

PSALM 16:11

The ordinary group of worshiping Christians, as the preacher sees them from the pulpit, does not look like a collection of very joyful people, in fact, they look on the whole rather sad, tired, depressed people. It is certain that such people will never win the world for Christ ...

It is no use trying to pretend: we may speak of joy and preach about it: but, unless we really have the joy of Christ in our hearts and manifest it, our words will carry no conviction to our hearers.

~ S. Neill

Lord, help us to be conscious

of how we portray You and let

us begin by looking at our inward

person. Then, let us spring forth

with the joy of the Lord. *Amen*

It's There!

Our citizenship is in heaven.
PHILIPPIANS 3:20

Elisabeth Elliot said, "Heaven is not here, it's There. If we were given all we wanted here, our hearts would settle for this world rather than the next. God is forever luring us up and away from this one, wooing us to Himself and His still invisible Kingdom, where we will certainly find what we so keenly long for."

Ecclesiastes 5:2 reminds us, "Do not be hasty in word or impulsive in thought to bring up a matter in the presence of God. For God is in heaven and you are on earth; therefore let your words be few."

We, who are born again, look forward
to going to heaven to our new home to spend
eternity with You, Father. Help us to do
what You ask us here on earth with the right
attitudes as we wait for the day when we will
go home to the celestial city. *Amen*

June 17

Liberty

*Now the Lord is the Spirit, and where
the Spirit of the Lord is, there is liberty.*
2 CORINTHIANS 3:17

This concern for the rights and liberties and welfare of the backward peoples is rooted in the Christian ethic of justice and of the duty to help and protect the weak, upon the Christian valuation of man as of spiritual dignity and worth, as made for freedom, as a potential child of God. These principles have no validity unless the Christian view of man be true.

~ Nathaniel Micklem

President Thomas Jefferson said of liberty: "God who gave us life gave us liberty. Can the liberties of a nation be secure when we have removed a conviction that these liberties are the gift of God?"

Thank You, Father, for our liberty.

Remind us of the great price that was paid for it.

Liberty, how blessed we are to have you. *Amen*

June 18

What a Gift!

Forever, O LORD, Your word is settled in heaven.
PSALM 119:89 NKJV

I believe the Bible is the best gift God has ever given to men. All the good from the Savior of the world is communicated to us through this Book ...

I have been driven many times to my knees by the overwhelming conviction that I had nowhere else to go.

~ Abraham Lincoln

Thank You, Lord God, for Your Word.

Let it be unto us the light to our path, and

the guide to our lives that You intended it to be.

Help us never to take it for granted. *Amen*

June 19

Sovereign Lord

He chose us in Him before the foundation of the world,
that we should be holy and without blame
before Him in love, having predestined us
to adoption as sons by Jesus Christ to Himself,
according to the good pleasure of His will.

EPHESIANS 1:4-5 NKJV

God will not hold us responsible to understand the mysteries of election, predestination, and the divine sovereignty.

The best and safest way to deal with these truths is to raise our eyes to God and in deepest reverence say, "O Lord, Thou knowest." Those things belong to the deep and mysterious profound of God's omniscience. Prying into them may make theologians, but it will never make saints.

~ A. W. Tozer

You, Lord God, are sovereign and have
known everything from the beginning of time.
May we always be mindful of
Your greatness and majesty. *Amen*

This Man, Jesus

You will conceive and give birth to a Son,
and you are to call Him Jesus.
LUKE 1:31 NIV

Is it any wonder that the priests realized that between this Man and themselves there was no choice but that He or priestcraft should perish? Is it any wonder that the Roman soldiers, confronted and amazed by something soaring over their comprehension and threatening all their disciplines, should take refuge in wild laughter, and crown Him with thorns and robe Him in purple and make a mock Caesar of Him?

For to take Him seriously was to enter upon a strange and alarming life, to abandon habits, to control instincts and impulses, to essay an incredible happiness ... Is it any wonder that to this day this Galilean is too much for our small hearts?

~ H. G. Wells

As we bow before You, Jesus,
may we always be children that bless
Your wonderful name. *Amen*

Choose Obedience

"See, I have set before you today life and good, death and evil, in that I command you today to love the LORD your God, to walk in His ways, and to keep His commandments, His statutes, and His judgments, that you may live and multiply; and the LORD your God will bless you in the land which you go to possess."

DEUTERONOMY 30:15-16 NKJV

God's revelations are sealed to us until they are opened to us by obedience. You will never get them open by philosophy or thinking. Immediately you obey, a flash of light comes. Let God's truth work in you by soaking in it, not by worrying into it. Obey God in the thing He is at present showing you, and instantly the next thing is opened up ... We say, "I suppose I shall understand these things someday."

You can understand them now: it is not study that does it, but obedience. The tiniest fragment of obedience, and heaven opens up and the profoundest truths of God are yours straightaway. God will never reveal more truth about Himself till you obey what you know already. Beware of being wise and prudent.

~ Oswald Chambers

Help us to always obey You, Lord. *Amen*

June 22

Anxious for Nothing

Be anxious for nothing, but in everything
by prayer and supplication with thanksgiving
let your request be made known to God.

PHILIPPIANS 4:6

Remember, you are destined for the throne! God is training you now. Your trials are not an accident: no suffering is purposeless. Your eternal profit is in view. Therefore, don't waste your sorrows!

~ Paul E. Billheimer

Father, our lives have so much in them
that we tend to get anxious over the
most mundane things. Lord,
help us to run to You in prayer
at the slightest impression of anxiety.
Break us from allowing this
enemy to rob us of our joy. *Amen*

A Future Hope in Believing

*In Scripture it says: "See, I lay a stone in Zion,
a chosen and precious cornerstone, and the
one who trusts in Him will never be put to shame."*

1 PETER 2:6 NIV

God the Father, Son, and Holy Ghost isn't a consulting firm we bring in to give us expert advice on how to run our lives.

The gospel life isn't something we learn about and then put together with instructions from the manufacturer; it's something we become as God does His work of creation and salvation in us and as we accustom ourselves to a life of belief and obedience and prayer.

~ Eugene H. Peterson

God, You have brought into existence
all that we know and much that we will
not know until we sit with You in glory.
Help our belief and, Lord,
help our unbelief. *Amen*

A New Heart

*"I will give you a new heart and
put a new spirit within you."*
EZEKIEL 36:26 NKJV

To break the basic laws of justice and decency is sin indeed. Man's freedom to honor principles is the moral dimension in his nature, and sin often appears as lawlessness. But sin has its roots in something which is more than the will to break the law. The core of sin is our making ourselves the center of life, rather than accepting the holy God as the center.

Lack of trust, self-love, pride – these are three ways in which Christians have expressed the real meaning of sin. But what sin does is to make the struggle with evil meaningless. When we refuse to hold our freedom in trust and reverence for God's will, there is nothing which can make the risk of life worth the pain of it.

~ Daniel Day Williams

Sin has no dominion over God's children.
Thank You for this truth, Lord. *Amen*

The Whole Bible

*"If even salt has become tasteless,
with what will it be seasoned?"*

LUKE 14:34

Owing to the pressure of an ever-increasing number of subjects introduced into the curriculum of a school, it is only too possible for men to be held to be educated and intelligent without ever having seriously tested their intelligence upon, say, the Book of Job, or upon the Epistle of Paul to the Romans.

But is quite certain that a widespread relaxation of the tension of biblical interpretation has disastrous effects. For there is no corruption that threatens a country so surely as the corruption or sentimentalizing of its religion; and there is no corruption of the Christian religion so swift as that which sets in when the Church loses its strict biblical discipline.

~ E. C. Hoskyns

Draw us to our knees as we plead
with You, Father, to teach us to
obey the whole Bible. *Amen*

June 26

The Best Gift

"If you then, being evil, know how to give good gifts to your children, how much more will your Father who is in heaven give good things to those who ask Him!"
MATTHEW 7:11 NKJV

Most parents will do whatever they can to provide exactly what their children want for special occasions such as a birthday or Christmas. It brings a sense of joy to bless our children while watching them spend fun-filled hours enjoying the item they so wanted.

God loves our children more than we ever could and He wants to bless them with gifts that we can't even imagine ... with His gifts come joy unspeakable, and life for all eternity. It is important, then, that we parents help our children to know Christ at an early age and to understand His promises to them. He gives the best gifts of all and His resources are limitless.

Thank You, Father, for the gift of eternal life.
Amen

June 27

Infinitely Valuable

Keep me as the apple of Your eye;
hide me under the shadow of Your wings.

PSALM 17:8 NKJV

Many times in our lives we are dropped, crumpled and ground into the dirt by the decisions we make and the circumstances that come our way. We feel as though we are worthless.

No matter what has happened or what will happen, we will never lose our value in God's eyes. To Him, dirty or clean, crumpled or finely creased, we are still priceless to Him. We can rest assured that He is always available to us and that He desires to commune with us.

Father, we have value because
we are created in Your image.
I pray that we will never forget
who we are in Christ Jesus. *Amen*

June 28

A Choice Jewel

The LORD is for me; I will not fear;
what can man do to me?
PSALM 118:6

Christian, let God's distinguishing love to you mo-
tivate you to fear Him greatly. He has put His fear
in your heart, and may not have given that blessing
to your neighbor, perhaps not to your husband; your
wife, your child, or your parent.

Oh, what an obligation should this thought lay
upon your heart to greatly fear the Lord! Remember
also that this fear of the Lord is His treasure, a choice
jewel, given only to favorites, and to those who are
greatly beloved.

~ John Bunyan

Father, You are our Protector.
We put our trust in You as we
understand that we are only to
have a reverent fear of the Lord,
for mere man can do nothing to us. *Amen*

June 29

Being Accountable

*"What will it profit a man if he
gains the whole world, and loses his own soul?"*

MARK 8:36 NKJV

Jesus taught that possessions must always be regarded as a secret trust. Every person is accountable to God for the use which they make of material goods. Everything we have is from God. We are all God's stewards.

Nothing is more certain to bring God's judgment and condemnation in the end than a selfish attitude toward the good things of this world. Jesus always insisted that if a person's possessions are beginning to injure their soul, drastic sacrifices are necessary. It is better to cut off a right hand than to quench the Spirit; and better to go into the kingdom of heaven a pauper, rather than die rich with a pile of gold and a shriveled, beggared soul.

Lord, help us to not hold on to things,
but to be held accountable for what You bless us with,
to be used for all the right purposes. *Amen*

June 30

No Substitutes

Don't copy the behavior and customs of this world,
but let God transform you into a new person.

ROMANS 12:2 NLT

We have been trying to apply machine-age methods to our relations with God. We read our chapter, have our short devotions, and rush away, hoping to make up for our deep inward bankruptcy by attending another gospel meeting or listening to another thrilling story told by a religious adventurer lately returned from afar. The tragic results of this spirit are all about us. Shallow lives, hollow religious philosophies, the preponderance of the element of fun in gospel meetings, the glorification of men, trust in religious externalities, quasi-religious fellowships, salesmanship methods, the mistaking of dynamic personality for the power of the Spirit; these and such as these are the symptoms of an evil disease, a deep and serious malady of the soul.

~ A. W. Tozer

Forgive us, Lord, for we have sinned. Thank You, Lord,

that we can re-enter fellowship with You.

Help us to make time with You a

priority every day. *Amen*

July

Fighting Temptation

"Keep watching and praying,
that you may not enter into temptation;
the spirit is willing, but the flesh is weak."

MATTHEW 26:41

What an awful trio of foes is arrayed against the Christian in temptation. There is the world; the flesh; and the devil. The world – the foe about us: the adversary – the foe beside us: the flesh – the foe within us. All of these combine in fierce assault upon the believer ... We must fly to our Lord in prayer. None else but Him has ever overcome this trinity of foes embattled against us. Only in His power through prayer can we prevail."

~ James McConkey

Lord, we cannot fight temptation
apart from You. We commit our lives
to You, O Lord, and pray that we
will come running when the tempter
comes in to subdue us. We call
upon Your name to be our strength.
We love You, Lord, and want
to stay pure for You. *Amen*

Times of Solitude

As for me, it is good to be near God.
I have made the Sovereign LORD my refuge.
PSALM 73:28 NIV

Modern civilization is so complex as to make the devotional life all but impossible. It wears us out by multiplying distractions and beats us down destroying our solitude, where otherwise we might drink and renew our strength, before going out to face the world again …

Where is the solitude to which we can retire today? "Commune with your own heart upon your bed and be still," is a wise and healing counsel. The need for solitude and quietness was never greater than it is today … the masses want it the way it is, and the majority of Christians are so completely conformed to this present age that they, too, want things the way they are. They may be annoyed a bit … but apparently they are not annoyed enough to do anything about it.

~ A. W. Tozer

Lord, turn our hearts toward You
in times of solitude. *Amen*

That All-Important First Step

He said, "Come!" And Peter got out of the boat, and walked on the water and came toward Jesus.
MATTHEW 14:29

B ut when once Christ had called him, Peter had no alternative – he must leave the ship and come to Him. In the end, the first step of obedience proves to be an act of faith in the word of Christ.

But we should completely misunderstand the nature of grace if we were to suppose that there was no need to take the first step, because faith was already there. Against that, we must boldly assert that the step of obedience must be taken before faith can be possible. Unless he obeys, a man cannot believe.

~ Dietrich Bonhoeffer

Help us, Lord, to be in such a close relationship with You that we do not falter when we step out onto the waters You tell us to walk on. *Amen*

July 4

The Race of Life

The path of the just is like the shining sun,
that shines ever brighter unto the perfect day.
PROVERBS 4:18 NKJV

God wants His highest for us, but we must not sit back and expect it to be handed to us on a silver platter. We must set goals and reach for new heights. We have work to do here on planet earth. There is a race to run: a race God has set before us.

Philippians 3:14-16 admonishes us to "press on toward the goal for the prize of the upward call of God in Christ Jesus. Let us therefore, as many as are perfect, have this attitude; and if in anything you have a different attitude, God will reveal that also to you; however, let us keep living by that same standard to which we have attained."

Help us as we run the race
of this Christian life. *Amen*

Ivy Cannot Grow Alone

*Blessed is the man who walks not
in the counsel of the ungodly.*

PSALM 1:1 NKJV

No man can be without his god. If he have not the true God to bless and sustain him, he will have some false god to delude and to betray him … Man was made to lean on the Creator; but if not on Him, then he leans on the creature in one shape or another.

The ivy cannot grow alone: it must twine round some support or other; if not the goodly oak, then the ragged thorn – round any dead stick whatever, rather than have no stay or support at all. It is even so with the heart and affections of man; if they do not twine around God, they must twine around some meaner thing.

~ Richard C. Trench

God, as we lean on You,
help us to learn from Your heart,
and Your Word. *Amen*

The Definition of Craftiness

We have renounced the things hidden because of shame, not walking in craftiness or adulterating the word of God, but by the manifestation of truth commending ourselves to every man's conscience in the sight of God.

2 CORINTHIANS 4:2

Fifteenth-century Ignatius Loyola explains craftiness: "As the devil showed great skill in tempting men to perdition, equal skill ought to be shown in saving them.

The devil studied the nature of each man, seized upon the traits of his soul, adjusted himself to them and insinuated himself gradually into his victim's confidence – suggesting splendors to the ambitious, gain to the covetous, delight to the sensuous, and a false appearance of piety to the pious – and a winner of souls ought to act in the same cautious and skillful way."

Jesus, we stand against the enemy of this world and proclaim that we know his ways, and that he has no power over us. *Amen*

July 7

Jesus' Success

The LORD your God will make you
abound in all the work of your hand.
DEUTERONOMY 30:9 NKJV

Jesus of Nazareth, without money and arms, conquered more millions than Alexander, Caesar, Mahomet, and Napoleon; without science and learning ... without the eloquence of schools, He spoke words of life such as never were spoken before or since, and produced effects which lie beyond the reach of any orator or poet; without writing a single line, He has set more pens in motion, and furnished themes for more sermons, orations, discussions, learned volumes, works of art and sweet songs of praise, than the whole army of great men of ancient and modern times ...

The annals of history produce no other example of such complete and astonishing success in spite of the absence of those material, social, literary, and artistic powers and influences which are indispensable to success for a mere man.

~ Philip Schaff

Lord, bless us and bless our labor. *Amen*

July 8

Hope for the Future

This hope we have as an anchor of the soul,
a hope both sure and steadfast
and one which enters within the veil.
HEBREWS 6:19

William White said, "I am not afraid of tomorrow for I have seen yesterday and I love today."

And John Oxenham elaborated on the subject a century ago with his comments: "Some people are reluctant to consider the future, arguing that it must be left to solve its own problems and to shape its own beliefs. In all right efforts for the future, religion must be given first place.

No provision to secure peace or just social principles can be worth much unless the foremost aim be to establish the kingdom of God. It is not the minds and bodies only of generations to come that have to be remembered, but their immortal souls."

Father, help us to move
forward into the future with
hope in our hearts. *Amen*

July 9

Overcoming Adversity

You may grant him relief from the days of adversity.
PSALM 94:13

God's Word says that sorrow that is according to the will of God produces a repentance without regret, leading to salvation, but the sorrow of the world produces death. We see Christians going through adversity that they did nothing to create. God uses that adversity in their lives, and in the lives of others.

We can be overcomers. We cannot overlook the host of good programs that help rehabilitate people, but there is one sure way to get to the root of harmful adversity in our lives ... the answer comes at the foot of the cross of Christ. He is the only one who is able to help us overcome adversity. Prayerfully, we will be able to say, as did Christ when He hung on the cross, "Not My will, but Yours be done" (Luke 22:42).

Lord, help us to withstand
adversity and be victorious. *Amen*

July 10

Be Holy

*You are a people holy to the L*ORD *your God.*
Out of all the peoples on the face of the earth,
*the L*ORD *has chosen you to be His treasured possession.*

DEUTERONOMY 14:2 NIV

The deepest need of men is not food and clothing and shelter, important as they are. It is God. We have mistaken the nature of poverty, and thought it was economic poverty. No, it is poverty of soul, deprivation of God's re-creating, loving peace.

Peer into poverty and see if we are really getting down to the deepest needs, in our economic salvation schemes. These are important. But they lie farther along the road, secondary steps toward world reconstruction. The primary step is a holy life, transformed and radiant in the glory of God.

~ Thomas R. Kelly

We pray, Lord, that our lives will be blameless as we walk with You. Help us to seek You with our whole heart, desiring to serve every day honoring You, God, with lives that are intent on being holy. *Amen*

Consider Your Words

Do you see a man who is hasty in his words?
There is more hope for a fool than for him.
PROVERBS 29:20

L et the words of my mouth and the meditation of my heart be acceptable in Your sight, O LORD, my rock and my Redeemer" (Ps. 19:14). What a difficult lesson to learn. It is much the way of the world to blurt out whatever comes to mind, often without regard to the pain inflicted. Each of us has been the recipient of hurtful words spoken by someone in haste … and just as many times, said hurtful things that cut to the core ourselves.

Often cutting words are not spoken with hurtful intentions. The Christian's position is to build up and edify, and to search out the wounded in the body of Christ and help them in their restoration.

Help us, Father, to build up and edify

as we offer comfort and compassion

to the wounded around us. *Amen*

Glory Through Suffering

We also glory in tribulations, knowing that tribulation produces perseverance; and perseverance, character; and character, hope.

ROMANS 5:3-4 NJKV

Your suffering may not be as profound as someone else you know, but the level of suffering one experiences is painful to them, and it is real. God has it planned so that the period of suffering is there for a purpose; He will bless us in it and out of it in His timing.

When we look at suffering the way Christ intended us to, we can rest, even though the suffering is still going on all around us. He is mighty and able to handle all our suffering. We can be overcomers, as Helen Keller once said, "Although the world is full of suffering, it is also full of the overcoming of it."

Lord, help us to allow You to work through our suffering. *Amen*

A Crown of Thorns

He gave up His divine privileges;
He took the humble position of a slave
and was born as a human being.

PHILIPPIANS 2:7 NLT

We need our visions for inspiration, but we must work in comparative shadow; otherwise, the very highest revelations would become monotonous, and we should long for still higher. And yet, are there not some whose desire is for constant revelation? Who would see supernatural sights, and hear supernatural sounds, and know all the realities towards which they are drifting, as well as those in which they must work?

They would make this world a mount of perpetual vision; overlooking the fact that it has its own purposes, to be wrought out by its own light, and within its own limits.

~ E. H. Chapin

Lord, we pray that we would
see the truth of all You
desire to show us and that we
would not be misled. *Amen*

Christ Is the Only Way

*"You are unwilling to come to
Me so that you may have life."*

JOHN 5:40

This uniqueness of Jesus Christ involves, as a necessary consequence, that to Him all other men must resort if they would find the secret and power of victory, order and peace; for He stands forth the solitary Man who ever held that secret, secured that victory, enjoyed that peace.

There never has been any other person who has saved sinners from their sins, or was entitled to say: I am the Light upon all your problems; come unto Me and I will give you rest from disorder and disaster. God sent forth His Son to be the Savior of the world, and there is none other. Man must fix his attention upon Christ, as an Object outside of himself, if order is ever to reign within himself.

~ G. H. Lang

Savior, help us to come to You
with hearts ready to be
transformed by Your love
and grace. *Amen*

July 15

The Invitation

"Come, for all things are now ready."
LUKE 14:17 NKJV

If the reason why a sinner is to come is because all things are ready, then it is idle for him to say, "But I am not ready." It is clear that all the readiness required on man's part is a willingness to come and receive the blessing which God has provided. There is nothing else necessary; if men are willing to come, they may come, they will come.

Where the Lord has been pleased to touch the will so that man has a desire towards Christ, where the heart really hungers and thirsts after righteousness, that is all the readiness which is wanted.

~ Charles H. Spurgeon

Thank You, Father, for the preparation
You have made. Help us to enter
in and abide in You. *Amen*

New Heights

*God has not given us a spirit of fear,
but of power and of love and of sound mind.*
2 TIMOTHY 1:7 NKJV

We may be able to help elevate the morale of someone for a while, but they will feel the effects of the scale sliding to the left again soon unless there is some real substance rather than a momentary boost. God is the one who causes morale to soar to new heights.

When we understand and accept that Christ is Lord and He is the way to eternal life, and also to a life of joy and contentment, we will then get a high that will last ... high that has more than a buzz ... a high we can enthusiastically share with our families, friends, and coworkers ... a high only Christ can give.

Lord, help us to look to You for what
we need to give us the boosts
we need to keep moving
forward and upward. *Amen*

July 77

Baseball!

... We beheld His glory.
JOHN 1:14 NKJV

Roger Angell said, "Any baseball is beautiful. No other small package comes as close to the ideal in design and utility: a perfect object for a man's hand. Pick it up and it instantly suggests its purpose: it is meant to be thrown a considerable distance — thrown hard and with precision. Its feel and heft are the beginning of the sport's critical dimensions; if it were a fraction of an inch larger or smaller, a few centigrams heavier or lighter, the game of baseball would be utterly different."

The Bible is beautiful. No other small package comes as close to the ideal in design and utility. Pick it up and it instantly suggests its purpose: it is meant to be read with a desire to know the Author.

Help us, Father, to sit at Your feet and learn from You so that we may be the sweet aroma of Christ to a lost world. *Amen*

July 18

The Game Has Begun

... Full of grace and truth.
JOHN 1:14

Roger Angell continued and said, "Hold a baseball in your hand ... Feel the ball, turn it over in your hand; hold it across the seam or the other way, with the seam just to the side of your middle finger. Speculation stirs. You want to get outdoors and throw this spare and sensual object to somebody or, at the very least, watch somebody else throw it. The game has begun."

Hold the Bible in your hand ... flip through its pages. Read it. Your heart pounds as you learn who Christ is and that He came to this earth to live and die so we could have a life spent in eternity with Him.

The Bible draws us to its truths. Share it with another lost soul and watch as they come to know Christ. The Christian life has begun.

Lord, help us to love Your Word
and to share it with others. *Amen*

July 19

God's Principles in Business

Some went out on the sea in ships; they were merchants on the mighty waters. They saw the works of the LORD, His wonderful deeds in the deep.
PSALM 107:23-24 NIV

Thomas J. Watson said, "Whenever an individual, or a business, decides that success has been attained, progress stops." God has given every instruction we need to operate a business in the Bible. One area He mentions many times is the area of pride. There is no room for pride in business, which includes many practices labeled "competitive."

Every business, even the church in a sense, is competitive as they seek to make theirs the best and most attractive. Good, well-planned and effective advertising practices should not include destructive motives. When God's principles for operating a business are in place, He is the One who will make it work to the point of great success.

God, may Christian men and women in business
give You Your rightful place as the Chief
Operation Officer of their businesses. *Amen*

Members of One Body

You are no longer strangers and aliens,
but you are fellow citizens with the saints,
and are of God's household.

EPHESIANS 2:19

God is not satisfied with single, separate Christians. When we believe on the Lord and partook of Him we became members of His body. Oh that God would cause this fact to break upon us!

Do I seek spiritual experiences for myself? Do I make converts for my denomination? Or have I caught the wisdom of the one heavenly Man, and realized that God is seeking to bring men into that?

When I do, salvation, deliverance, inducement with the Spirit, yes, everything in Christian experience will be seen from a new viewpoint, everything for me will be transformed.

~ Watchman Nee

Father, shake us up and move
us to where we can be used by You
for Your kingdom's work. *Amen*

Steps of Faith

For now we see in a mirror, dimly,
but then face to face. Now I know in part,
but then I shall know just as I also am known.
1 CORINTHIANS 13:12 NKJV

Sanctification is both a sudden step of faith, and also a gradual process of works. It is a step as far as we are concerned; it is a process as to God's part.

By a step of faith we get into Christ; by a process we are made to grow up unto Him in all things. By a step of faith we put ourselves into the hands of the Divine Potter; by a gradual process He makes us into a vessel unto His own honor, meet for His use, and prepared to every good work.

~ Hannah Whitall Smith

As our desire is to be like You,
Lord, may we be obedient to
Your Word so that we will grow
in faith to be like You. *Amen*

July 22

The Blessed Life

As many as received Him,
to them He gave the right to
become children of God,
to those who believe in His name:
who were born, not of blood,
nor of the will of the flesh,
nor of the will of man, but of God.

JOHN 1:12-13 NKJV

The *blessed life* should be the normal life of every Christian – in work and rest, in the building up of the inner life, and in the working out of the life plan. It is God's thought not for a few, but for all His children.

The youngest and weakest may lay claim to it equally with the strongest and oldest. We should step into it at the moment of conversion without wandering with blistered feet for forty years in the desert, or lying for thirty-eight years, with disappointed hopes, in the porch of the House of Mercy.

~ F. B. Meyer

Lord, You provided this new
and blessed life that is a blessing
beyond any words we can
express. Thank You. *Amen*

July 23

Loving Relationships

Therefore, as God's chosen people, holy and dearly loved, clothe yourselves with compassion, kindness, humility, gentleness and patience.

COLOSSIANS 3:12 NIV

Writer Og Mandino talks about death this way: "Beginning today," he said, "treat everyone you meet as if he or she were going to be dead by midnight.

Extend to them all the care, kindness, and understanding you can muster, and do so with no thought of any reward. Your life will never be the same again."

Lord, to love and to express love is not so simple at times, but You are love and You express Your love to us daily. We pray that we would learn from You, Father, in this area to make Your love the basis for building relationships and maintaining them. *Amen*

The Struggles of Life

*Those who wait for the L**ORD** will gain new strength;*
they will mount up with wings like eagles,
they will run and not get tired,
they will walk and not become weary.

ISAIAH 40:31

The struggle the butterfly must go through in order to break away from its cocoon and what a baby chick must endure as it pecks through its shell is what makes them whole. Sometimes struggles are exactly what we need in our life.

Struggle is not always a bad thing. God's plans are perfect and we must not interfere with the struggle of another, unless we are certain God wants us to reach out and assist them. If God allowed us to go through all our life without any obstacles, that would cripple us. We would not be as strong as what we could have been. Not only that, we could never fly.

God, thank You for giving us the resources we need to help us soar high above the obstacles we will surely face as Christians. *Amen*

July 25

The Issue of Pride

"You like to appear righteous in public,
but God knows your hearts.
What this world honors is detestable
in the sight of God."
LUKE 16:15 NLT

Teaching children that pride is a destructive part of many adult lives and teaching how to combat the issue of pride early in life is no easy task for any parent. So many of us were not taught such important lessons as children. Consequently, we are still in the struggling stages ourselves. The sooner we recognize pride in our own lives, the sooner we can train our children by example. Pride is a destructive attitude and should be confessed the moment it surfaces in the life of Christians of any age.

Lord, forgive us for not accepting those things
You have for us that will make us more like You.
Help us to allow You to move in us and
in those we love according to Your perfect plan,
even when that plan doesn't look the way
we think it should. Help us to overcome
the sin of pride, we pray. *Amen*

July 26

Daily Ministry

The LORD will wait, that He may be gracious to you;
and therefore He will be exalted,
that He may have mercy on you.
For the Lord is a God of justice;
blessed are all those who wait for Him.
ISAIAH 30:18 NKJV

Acceptance of those on a foreign field, in the pastorate, or in some position with a title as "in ministry" is easy. However, all Christians are in ministry, every day, no matter what our title or where we serve: We are all called to a place of service. That place might be as a homemaker, the caregiver of a loved one, a factory worker, a receptionist, etc.

It makes no difference where we are. As children of God, we are called to be witnesses of the Gospel of Christ. Christians are missionaries commissioned to spread the Gospel to the lost world around us.

Lord, You called us to bear witness
to You by spreading the Gospel
truth. Help us to do so. *Amen*

Holy Communion

If you would prepare your heart,
and stretch out your hands toward Him.
JOB 11:13 KJV

Man obtains nothing without laying out time upon it. Even where free grace is to do everything apart from our working, we must give it time to carry out its work in our hearts. It is only when in secrecy I resolve with myself to look to Jesus until my desires become truly operative within me, that I shall be really prepared for the banquet.

It is only when I deal trustfully with Him in the ordinary converse of the hidden and the daily life, that I can expect extraordinary blessing from public communion with Him at His table. Yea, hunger and thirst cannot be awakened simply when I see the table. It is in the conflict of the preceding life that hunger and thirst are aroused. Only for such is the table a feast. May this quickening not be wanting to me in this preparation.

~ Andrew Murray

Lord, prepare us for Holy Communion. *Amen*

July 28

The Lord's Temple

We are the temple of the living God.
2 CORINTHIANS 6:16

We build our lives in a distracted way, reacting rather than acting, willing to put up less than the best. At important points we do not give the job our best effort. Then with a shock we look at the situation we have created and find that we are now living in the house we have built. If we had realized that, we would have done it differently.

Think of yourself as the carpenter. Think about your house. Each day you hammer a nail, place a board, or erect a wall. Build wisely. It is the only life you will ever build. Even if you live it for only one day more, that day deserves to be lived graciously and with dignity. The plaque on the wall says, "Life is a do-it-yourself project." Your life tomorrow will be the result of your attitudes and the choices you make today.

Help us, God, to keep our temple
in exceptional condition. *Amen*

Jesus, the True Vine

"I am the vine, you are the branches."

JOHN 15:5

All earthly things are the shadows of heavenly realities – the expression, in created, visible forms, of the invisible glory of God ... How many eyes have gazed on and admired a great vine with its beautiful fruit? Come and gaze on the heavenly Vine till your eye turns from all else to admire Him.

How many, in a sunny climate, sit and rest under the shadow of a vine? Come and be still under the shadow of the true Vine, and rest under it from the heat of the day. What countless numbers rejoice in the fruit of the vine! Come, and take, and eat of the heavenly fruit of the true Vine, and let your soul say: "I sat under His shadow with great delight, and His fruit was sweet to my taste."

~ Andrew Murray

Father, may we draw from You
daily what we need to mature into
godly men and women. *Amen*

The Greatest Love

"Greater love has no one than this,
that one lay down his life for his friends."

JOHN 15:13

Accounts of people who willingly donate one of their organs to make certain a friend or family member can live longer and in a body virtually free of pain tugs at our hearts. We are happy for the one who received the organ while surprised, and grateful, to the one who made the contribution, often risking their own life.

God gave not just an organ, but He gave His only begotten Son's life, that we might have life for all eternity. So many are still not moved enough to accept this wonderful gift. Think about it: eternity with Christ, in exchange for the old body we now have!

God, help us to love others more than the self,
and help us to love You enough to accept You
and the price You paid for our lives. *Amen*

July 31

The Four-Way Test

The integrity of the upright will guide them.
PROVERBS 11:3

The business philosophy is a simple four-step decision-making tool. It didn't tell people what to do or how to think, but it did give them a tool to use in all of their business dealings. The tool is now well known to anyone that has ever associated themselves with Rotary International. It is called "the four-way test."

The four-way test asks these four questions: Is it the *truth*? Is it *fair* to all concerned? Will it build *goodwill* and better friendships? Will it be *beneficial* to all concerned? The tip is to use this simple decision-making tool in your life and see what a difference it makes. As people, we must all stand by our personal honesty and integrity. This is a handy and simple test of what you say, do or think. Give it a try.

Lord, help us to become people of honesty and integrity. *Amen*

August

August 1

Living by Example

I also do my best to maintain always a blameless conscience both before God and before men.

ACTS 24:16

Someone is always watching us, so our behavior is a living example of the God we love and serve. We must make certain that we wear our Christianity in a manner that honors the Lord and so that the lost will want to know Him. It is equally as important that we be aware of not causing a Christian sibling to stumble or fall.

Dressing each day takes on a whole different meaning when we want to maintain a blameless conscience before God and people!

Awesome God, we want to be like You.
We need Your help as we represent
You every day, whether at home,
school, work or just out for some fun.
Thank You for Your example. *Amen*

August 2

Unwavering Faith

After you have suffered for a little while, the God of all grace, who called you to His eternal glory in Christ, will Himself perfect, confirm, strengthen and establish you.

1 PETER 5:10

George Müller stressed that we "do but stand still in the hour of trial, and you will see the help of God, if you trust in Him. But there is so often a forsaking the ways of the Lord in the hour of trial, and thus the food of faith, the means whereby our faith may be increased, is lost. As the increase of faith is a good gift, it must come from God, and therefore He ought to be asked for this blessing."

Nathaniel Hawthorne said, "Christian faith is a grand cathedral, with divinely pictured windows. Standing without, you can see no glory, nor can imagine any, but standing within, every ray of light reveals a harmony of unspeakable splendors."

God, as we learn to trust You with unwavering faith, may we know deep in the recesses of our hearts that You desire the same thing. *Amen*

August 3

Follow His Lead

A person's steps are directed by the LORD.
How then can anyone understand their own way?
PROVERBS 20:24 NIV

The popular poem known simply as *Footprints* has been around for many years. We don't know who the author is, but it is certain they had an understanding of God's concern for the direction we choose to take in life.

We are told in Proverbs that our steps are ordered by Him. When we don't allow Him to guide us, we walk in circles and even lose our way. Christ had a plan for us before we were born. How wonderful it would be if we would allow Him to do what He is a master at ... lead us, and even carry us, when we need Him to. He is always ready and willing to show us the way.

Lord, You have a master plan for our lives already prepared. Guide us, we pray, so that we would follow Your lead. *Amen*

August 4

Disabled, but Not Unable

O God, You have taught me from my youth;
and to this day I declare Your wondrous works.
PSALM 71:17 NKJV

Children with disabilities stir emotions. They are often stared at, laughed at, ostracized, ignored, abused and left to fend for themselves. Many carry scars into their adult years from the horrible treatment received as children. Some become bitter and end up facing legal problems that often send them to jail or prison where the bad treatment and behavior continues.

Like any other person, when the disabled are accepted, loved, have their needs met and are properly challenged to become independent, they are successful, happy and active in their personal and community lives. It is our choice to encourage the disabled by accepting them, loving them, encouraging them and by being living examples of God's love.

God, bless those with disabilities and keep them in Your special care. Thank You for Your redeeming love that overcomes our infirmities. *Amen*

A Knee Meeting

Do not wear yourself out to get rich;
do not trust your own cleverness.
Cast but a glance at riches, and they are gone.

PROVERBS 23:4-5 NIV

The Lord tells people to work and to care for our families. However, when work consistently takes away from family time and time alone with Christ, there needs to be a meeting … a knee meeting … praying and seeking some answers from the Father above.

He always has time for His children. Never put your work above the Lord or your loved ones.

Jesus, You are always available to us.
Help us to honor and cherish our loved
ones in the same way. *Amen*

August 6

Cracked Vessels

You should clothe yourselves instead with the beauty that comes from within, the unfading beauty of a gentle and quiet spirit, which is so precious to God.

1 PETER 3:4 NLT

Each of us has our own unique flaws. We are all cracked pots. Don't be afraid of your flaws. Acknowledge them, and you, too, can be the cause of beauty. Know that in our weakness we find our strength.

Lord, may we desire to be meek in this earthly life so that You can use us in powerful ways to spread Your love and grace. May our lives be a living testament to Your overwhelming and transforming love. *Amen*

August 7

Christian Meditation

Let the words of my mouth and the meditation of my heart be acceptable in Your sight, O LORD, my strength and my Redeemer.

PSALM 19:14 NKJV

William Bridge said, "Meditation will keep your hearts and souls from sinful thoughts. When the vessel is full you can put in no more ... If the heart be full of sinful thoughts, there is no room for holy. If the heart be full of holy thoughts, there is no room for evil and sinful thoughts."

"And the peace of God, which surpasses all understanding, will guard your hearts and minds through Christ Jesus" (Philippians 4:7 NKJV).

Lord, "Peace, perfect peace, in this dark world of sin?

The blood of Jesus whispers peace within"

(Edward H. Bickersteth). *Amen*

Victory with Christ

If God is for us, who is against us?
ROMANS 8:31

The sermon delivered at the funeral of a minister who committed suicide describes the problems many of us incur when we come into the kingdom of God and think everything about us will automatically be changed into some fantasy world with no problems or concerns. This is certainly not what the Bible tells us: Christianity does not solve all of the problems we think it should solve.

Those who expected to be free of sinful habits and desires after a conversion in which "sudden victory" was promised may find themselves disillusioned with God altogether, when they realize that they are still sinners saved by grace. God didn't promise any of us health, wealth and happiness. In fact, He tells us that we who expect to share in Christ's glory will also participate in His suffering.

Lord, help us to understand the trials and tribulations we will encounter as Christians and to trust You through them. *Amen*

Precious Love

In this is love, not that we loved God,
but that He loved us.

1 JOHN 4:10 NKJV

Charles H. Spurgeon illustrates love in the most amazing way: "I wish, brothers and sisters, that we could all imitate 'the pearl oyster' – a hurtful particle intrudes itself into its shell, and this vexes and grieves it. It cannot reject the evil, but what does it do but 'cover' it with a precious substance extracted out of its own life, by which it turns the intruder into a pearl!

Oh, that we could do so with the provocations we receive from our fellow Christians, so that pearls of patience, gentleness, and forgiveness might be bred within us by that which otherwise would have harmed us."

God, we so need to learn to love with
the love You have freely given us.
As we struggle with our hardships,
help us to understand, accept
and walk in Your love. *Amen*

I Will Not Fear

Yea, though I walk through the valley of the shadow
of death, I will fear no evil; for You are with me;
Your rod and Your staff, they comfort me.

PSALM 23:4 NKJV

There is an essential difference between the decease of the godly and the death of the ungodly. Death comes to the ungodly man as a penal infliction, but to the righteous as a summons to his Father's palace.

To the sinner it is an execution, to the saint an undressing from his sins and infirmities. Death to the wicked is the king of terrors. Death to the saint is the end of terrors, the commencement of glory.

~ Charles H. Spurgeon

Father, Your death on the cross was so
ordered that we could have life eternal.
Help us not to be afraid of death,
for nothing can separate a born-again
believer from You. *Amen*

August 11

Our Creator God

You alone are the Lord. You have made the heavens,
the heaven of heavens with all their host,
the earth and all that is on it, the seas and
all that is in them. You give life to all of them
and the heavenly host bows down before You.

NEHEMIAH 9:6

Jesus Christ created all these things. 'It is He,' the Hebrews says, "that bringeth out their host by number." All these millions of galaxies He brought out and knows how many. He calls them all by names.

Again we see His omniscience. "By the greatness of His might, for that He is strong in power; not one faileth," or literally, "not one of these stars is missing." Isn't that amazing? Billions and quadrillions and infinite numbers of light years away there are stars which are hundreds and thousands of times larger than the earth, and they are still there. He has not lost one yet.

~ R. B. Thieme, Jr.

Thank You, God, for Your
amazing creation. *Amen*

August 12

God's Escape Hatch

Submit therefore to God. Resist the
devil and he will flee from you.

JAMES 4:7

Jesus provided a way of escape from the enemy, Satan. We can rest assured that there is a battle going on, but God fights for us. He is on our side. What more could anyone ask for?

If you are burdened by the weight of a heavy load of temptation, remember 1 Corinthians 10:13: "No temptation has overtaken you but such as is common to man; and God is faithful, who will not allow you to be tempted beyond what you are able, but with the temptation will provide the way of escape also, so that you will be able to endure it." Ask God to lead you through the escape hatch.

Lord, we are grateful that You have
made a way for us to flee the enemy,
and come to You. Thank You for every
detail of Your goodness to us. *Amen*

Take a Breather!

Rest in the LORD.
PSALM 37:7

Someone has said that modern life can be spelled in three words, "Hurry, worry, bury." One thinks of a senator who was asked, as he rushed breathlessly along, "What do you think of the world crises?"

He replied, "Don't bother me; I'm in a hurry to make a radio speech. A crisis like this leaves me no time to think!" The Bible has as much to say about resting as about working. Our Lord would have us come apart and rest awhile, for if we don't we will come apart!

~ Vance Havner

I pray, Father, that we would find time to sit back and enjoy what You have given to us. Keep us mindful of the importance of every minute of our time so that we will use our minutes wisely. *Amen*

August 14

The Battlefield

We are not fighting against flesh-and-blood enemies,
but against evil rulers and authorities of the unseen
world, against mighty powers in this dark world.
EPHESIANS 6:12 NLT

Catherine Marshall said, "Evil is real—and powerful. It has to be fought, not explained away, not fled. And God is against evil all the way. So each of us has to decide where we stand, how we're going to live our lives."

R. C. Holland, Jr. said, "There is no victory without the stench and heat of battle; there is no shining without burning. But when we finish our spiritual campaign in the battlefield of earth, we will stand before our Lord Jesus Christ and be pleasing to Him."

Lord, please help us lean on Your strength
for the battles we need to face. Thank You that
we can be assured of the victory. *Amen*

August 15

A Grim Reality

You have delivered my soul from death,
indeed my feet from stumbling, so that I may
walk before God in the light of the living.

PSALM 56:13

Thus it is in hell; they would die, but they cannot. The wicked shall be always dying but never dead; the smoke of the furnace descends for ever and ever. Oh! who can endure thus to be ever upon the rack? This word "ever" breaks the heart. Wicked men do now think the Sabbaths long, and think a prayer long; but oh! how long will it be to lie in hell for ever and ever?

The torments of hell abide for ever ... If all the earth and sea were sand, and every thousandth year a bird should come, and take away one grain of this sand, it would be a long time ere that vast heap of sand were emptied; yet, if after all that time the damned may come out of hell, there were some hope; but this word "ever" breaks the heart.

~ Thomas Watson

Thank You, Father, for Your atoning blood. *Amen*

August 16

Good Men and Women

The execution of justice is joy for the righteous,
but is terror to the workers of iniquity.
PROVERBS 21:15

Herman Wouk said, "Heroes are not supermen, they're good men, and embodied by the cast of destiny, the virtue of a whole people in a great hour."

And writing of the thousands of such heroes in our nation, men and women who wear our country's uniform in this troubled peace of ours, Ronald Reagan asked us to never forget "to reassure them that their hard, long training is needed, that love of country is noble, that self-sacrifice is rewarding, that to be ready to fight for freedom fills a man with a sense of worth like nothing else.

America is still the great beacon in dense gloom, with the promise to hundreds of millions of the oppressed that liberty exists, that it is the shining future, that they can throw off their tyrants, and learn freedom and cease learning war. So we still need heroes to stand guard in the night."

Lord, bless all those who
serve our country. *Amen*

August 17

To the Point

"Whatever you ask in My name, that will I do,
so that the Father may be glorified in the Son."
JOHN 14:13

A deacon from a small town was going on a business trip to the city for a week. He was asked to purchase a motto for the front of the church while he was there. Upon arriving in the city he discovered he had forgotten both the motto and the measurements, and so he wired a message for his wife to send them to him.

Who can blame the telegraph operator, who had just come in from luncheon and had not sent the first message, for fainting, for the telegram read: "Unto us a child is born, six feet long and five feet wide!" The wife did exactly what was asked, even though in few words.

Father, help us to learn to say, with few words,

what is most important for others to hear ...

the Gospel message. *Amen*

August 18

Work and Eat

If anyone is not willing to work,
then he is not to eat, either.
2 THESSALONIANS 3:10

The Bible clearly says that if one does not work, they should not eat. The Great Depression brought barren years, and people learned the importance of hard work. In the twenty-first century, there are those who have little or no understanding about where their food actually comes from or what it takes to make certain it is available: it is subconsciously assumed that it will be there.

Some of us recall times when very little food was available and if we did not plan well in the summer and harvest all we could to be canned or frozen, we knew we would face certain times of want around February of the next year. Hunger is an amazing driving force to make people work to feed themselves and their families.

Father, we pray we will see Your provision
every day as You help us to do our part in Your
perfect plan for that provision. *Amen*

Our Real Provider

Aspire to lead a quiet life, to mind your own business,
and to work with your own hands.

1 THESSALONIANS 4:11 NKJV

Many today have little or no understanding about working to make certain that there is food on the table. Food has just always been there. The Bible tells us that God's children need not beg for bread (see Ps. 37:25), which leads us to believe there are times when we cannot work. Hard-working men and women do get laid off from their jobs, they do have major illnesses that prevent them from working, and there are other legitimate reasons why a person may be unable to work for a time. God wants us to know that He is our real provider.

He is the one who allows circumstances in our lives to help us to trust Him and to help the church to recognize need and to respond to that need. God made provision for our daily needs, but He tells us to work.

God, thank You for Your provision. *Amen*

The Compassionate Christ

Jesus had compassion on them.
MATTHEW 20:34 NIV

No matter how low down you are; no matter what your disposition has been; you may be low in your thoughts, words, and actions; you may be selfish; your heart may be overflowing with corruption and wickedness; yet Jesus will have compassion upon you.

He will speak comforting words to you; not treat you coldly or spurn you, as perhaps those of earth would, but will speak tender words, and words of love and affection and kindness. Just come at once. He is a faithful Friend – a Friend that sticketh closer than a brother.

~ Dwight L. Moody

Compassionate Father, we love You, and thank You for Your tender heart toward us. *Amen*

August 21

The Real You

We destroy every proud obstacle that keeps people from knowing God. We capture their rebellious thoughts and teach them to obey Christ.

2 CORINTHIANS 10:5 NLT

It has been said that character is what we do when we are in the dark or when no one else knows about it. With that in mind, we need to remember that Christians are never alone ... God is omnipresent and He knows what we do even in the dark places.

So, character is really what we do when we are real! And it makes no difference if we think we are alone or not. It is the real me! Character is like a tree, and reputation like its shadow. The shadow is what we think of it, the tree is the real thing.

Jesus, help us to possess the Character of Christ. Help us to allow You to break us to that point of innocence that You can use to develop the very nature of God in us. *Amen*

His Word Is Final!

All Scripture is God-breathed and is useful for teaching,
rebuking, correcting and training in righteousness,
so that the servant of God may be
thoroughly equipped for every good work.

2 TIMOTHY 3:16-17 NIV

Now, I find a great many people who want some evidence that they have accepted the Son of God. My friends, if you want any evidence, take God's word for it. You can't find better evidence than that. You know that when the Angel Gabriel came down and told Zachariah he should have a son he wanted a further token than the angel's word.

He asked Gabriel for it and he answered, "I am Gabriel, who stands in the presence of the Lord." He had never been doubted, and he thundered out this to Zechariah. But he wanted a further token, and Gabriel said, "You shall have a token: you shall be dumb till your son shall be given you."

~ Dwight L. Moody

Father, Your Word is the manual we are to love and live by. We pray that it would become the most important of all our earthly possessions. *Amen*

Riches to Rags

He who trusts in his riches will fall,
but the righteous will flourish like foliage.
PROVERBS 11:28 NKJV

One day a father and his rich family took his son on a trip to the country with the firm purpose to show him how poor people can be. They spent a day and a night on the farm of a very poor family. When they got back from their trip the father asked his son, "How was the trip?" "Very good, Dad!" "Did you see how poor people can be?" the father asked. "Yeah!" "And what did you learn?"

The son answered, "I saw that we have a dog at home, and they have four. We have a pool that reaches to the middle of the garden, they have a creek that has no end. We have imported lamps in the garden, they have the stars. Our patio reaches to the front yard, they have a whole horizon." When the little boy was finishing, his father was speechless. His son added, "Thanks, Dad, for showing me how poor we are!"

Lord, help us to recognize and care for the poor, and to be grateful for all You have blessed us with. *Amen*

August 24

Never Ashamed

For I am not ashamed of the gospel.
ROMANS 1:16 KJV

I may say with truth that there is only about one in ten who professes Christianity who will turn round and glorify God with a loud voice. Nine out of ten are still-born Christians. You never hear of them. If you press them hard with the question whether they are Christians, they might say, "Well, I hope so."

We never see it in their actions; we never see it in their lives. They might belong to the church you go to, but you never see them at the prayer meetings or taking any interest in the church affairs. They don't profess it among their fellows or in their business, and the result is that there are hundreds going on with a half hope, not sure whether their religion will stand them or not. It is our privilege to know that we are saved.

~ Dwight L. Moody

O Lord, we pray that we would never
be ashamed of the glorious Gospel of
Jesus Christ. Forgive us, Father, and help us
to boldly proclaim the truth. *Amen*

Choices and Consequences

Choose for yourselves this day whom you will serve.

JOSHUA 24:15 NKJV

We have been given choices to make in life. When we fail to make right choices, and choose to engage in wrong behavior, the consequences can be painful to us and many others and can last a lifetime. The suffering does not always go away when we recognize our wrong choices or when we say we are sorry.

Only Christ can direct us to make the right choices in life. His plans for us include eternal security and a clean slate when we get to heaven.

Father God, we call upon You to guide us as
we make so many decisions every day.
Lord, we want to please You with the choices
we make. Help us to put Your Word
in our hearts so we will be able to
discern Your will for us. *Amen*

August 26

All for Good

You intended to harm me,
but God intended it all for good.
GENESIS 50:20 NLT

I believe," said Dietrich Bonhoeffer who was martyred during Hitler's rule, "that God can and will bring good out of all things, even the most evil for this He needs men who will let all things work for the best in respect to them. I believe that in every trial God will give us as much power to resist as we need. But in order that we will rely on Him alone and not ourselves, He does not give it ahead of time. Such faith must overcome all anxiety about the future.

I believe that even our mistakes and errors are not in vain, and it is no harder for God to deal with them than with what we regard as our good deeds. I believe that God is no timeless fate, but that He waits for and answers upright prayer and responsible deeds."

Thank You, Lord, for working for our good and turning trials into triumphs. *Amen*

Worship and Bow Down

Oh come, let us worship and bow down;
let us kneel before the LORD our Maker.
For He is our God, and we are the people
of His pasture, and the sheep of His hand.

PSALM 95:6-7 NKJV

God is to be worshiped, and that according to His own will and appointment, is a principal branch of the law of our creation written in our hearts, the sense whereof is renewed in the second commandment; but the ways and means of that worship depend merely on God's sovereign pleasure and institution.

~ John Owen

What a privilege we have to be able to worship You, Lord, in freedom. Help us to do so from our hearts and lift You up to the highest place. *Amen*

A King's Ransom

For there is one God, and one mediator also between God and men, who gave Himself as a ransom for all.
1 TIMOTHY 2:5-6

When prisoners were bartered at the conclusion of a war, the exchange was not always simply man for man. An officer was of more value than a common soldier, and several soldiers might be redeemed by the surrender of one officer. For a woman of high rank or extraordinary beauty a still greater number of prisoners might be exchanged; and by giving up a king's son many might be redeemed.

So the sense of His own unique dignity and His peculiar relation to God is implied in the statement that Christ's life would redeem the lives of many. St. Paul expresses the truth still more boldly when he says that Jesus gave His life has a ransom "for all"; but the two phases come to the same thing; because the "many" spoken of by Jesus really includes "all" who are willing to avail themselves of the opportunity.

~ James Stalker

Thank You, Lord for this incredible ransom and for giving up Your Son so that we could be free. *Amen*

God's Witnesses

"You are My witnesses," declares the LORD, *"and My servant whom I have chosen, so that you may know and believe Me and understand that I am He."*

ISAIAH 43:10

Hannah Whitall Smith's son, who preceded her in death, said, "We are God's witnesses necessarily, because the world will not read the Bible, but they will read our lives; and that upon the report these give will very much depend their belief in the divine nature of the religion we possess.

This age is essentially an age of facts, and all scientific inquiries are being increasingly turned from theories to realities. If, therefore, our religion is to make any headway in the present time, it must be proved to be more than theory; and we must present to the investigation of the critical minds of our age the realities of lives transformed by the mighty power of God, 'working in them all the good pleasure of His will.'"

Help us, Lord God, to be holy and to be good witnesses in the world. *Amen*

The Real Thing

*Give me an eagerness for Your laws
rather than a love for money!*
PSALM 119:36 NLT

Until a couple of decades ago, most married couples had very little they could call their own when they married. My spouse and I could fit all our worldly possessions in our tiny car with one very small U-Haul carrier on the top. We had so much fun shopping for our first furniture ... all used, of course, and we loved painting and fixing it up. We had to be satisfied with what we had and who we were.

John Newton said, "I am not what I ought to be. I am not what I want to be. I am not what I hope to be. But still, I am not what I used to be. And by the grace of God, I am what I am."

Jesus, help us to be satisfied with what we have and who we are in You. *Amen*

He Knows Your Name

"Fear not, for I have redeemed you;
I have called you by your name; you are Mine."

ISAIAH 43:1 NKJV

God knew us by name in our mother's womb. He knows the number of hairs on our heads. He is intimately acquainted with our sorrows. He knows all about us. What a sweet expression of His love for us ... He knows us by name!

We, though, fail miserably at showing others that we even recognize them, much less take time to learn about them. Looking for people we normally pass each day without noticing would be a good lesson to learn this coming week. What a way to teach children about the love of God!

Your name is above all names, Lord God, and we worship You. Thank You, Lord, for showing us the value You place on Your children. Bless Your holy name.

Amen

September

Worth Dying For

I have been crucified with Christ;
it is no longer I who live, but Christ lives in me.

GALATIANS 2:20 NKJV

The story is told of two armed, hooded, Gestapo-like soldiers who entered an underground church in what was once communist Romania. With their guns in their hands they yelled, "We don't believe in your faith. Those who do not abandon it immediately will be shot at once! Now, those who wish to abandon it, move to the right!"

Some moved to the right. These were ordered to leave the church and go home. They fled for their lives. When the soldiers were alone with the remaining Christians, they took off their hoods, embraced them and told them, "We too are Christians, but we wished to have fellowship only with those who consider the truth worth dying for."

God, help us to be willing to take the first steps to understanding what faith worth dying for is all about. *Amen*

Making Waves

"I know the plans that I have for you,"
declares the LORD.

JEREMIAH 29:11

A small boy sailed his toy boat on a pond. The boat floated out of his reach, and he appealed to a larger boy to help him. This boy, without saying a word, picked up rocks and began throwing them out near the boat.

The small boy pleaded with him not to hit his boat, but the big boy kept on. Soon the small boy noticed that each stone was falling on the far side of the boat, making a wave that pushed it nearer to the shore. Then he realized that the big boy was planning the fall of each stone in order to bring the boat nearer. Soon it was within reach and the owner had his boat again.

We must never forget that God plans the fall of each stone within our circumstances, and that each storm and wave is calculated by Him in order to bring us nearer to Himself.

Jesus, Your plans are perfect
and for our good. *Amen*

Life's Greatest Meaning

Delight yourself in the LORD;
and He will give you the desires of your heart.
Commit your way to the LORD, trust also in Him.

PSALM 37:4-5

The great danger facing all of us ... is not that we shall make an absolute failure of life, nor that we shall fall into outright viciousness, nor that we shall be terribly unhappy, nor that we shall feel [that] life has no meaning at all – not these things.

The danger is that we may fail to perceive life's greatest meaning, fall short of its highest good, miss its deepest and most abiding happiness, be unable to tender the most needed service, be unconscious of life ablaze with the light of the presence of God – and be content to have it so – that is the danger ... For life without God, to one who has known the richness and joy of life with Him, is unthinkable, impossible. That is what one prays one's friends may be spared – satisfaction with a life that falls short of the best.

~ Phillips Brooks

Lord, may we be brought to that place
of intimate relationship with You and live
a joyful life of abundance. *Amen*

His Word Our Authority

Your word is a lamp for my feet,
a light on my path.

PSALM 119:105 NIV

We are to believe and follow Christ in all things, including His words about Scripture. And this means that Scripture is to be for us what it was to Him: the unique, authoritative, and inerrant Word of God, and not merely a human testimony to Christ, however carefully guided and preserved by God. If the Bible is less than this to us, we are not fully Christ's disciples.

~ James Montgomery Boice

We have Your Word on the matter, Lord God.

We know that the Bible is our ultimate authority.

Thank You for this amazing gift. *Amen*

Prove Him Great!

Great is the LORD, and greatly to be praised.
PSALM 145:3 NKJV

God knows the barriers we will face in marriage, but He can change any situation at any time. God can give a couple favor in the sight of foes. When God sends us to do a task, He gives enough promises to cover all difficulties and impossibilities. God doesn't ignore our doubts and fears, even though His promises deal with them, but meets them.

We cannot expect people to believe we are God's representatives unless "signs" are very evident. God will give "outward" signs of authority. God does not force Himself on us, but floods us with evidence until we believe, even though we might doubt at first. God is willing to prove Himself in us. The question remains, are we willing to allow Him room to prove Himself in and through us?

God, help us to allow You room
to work in our lives. *Amen*

September 6

Cutting Words

"Every careless word that people speak, they shall give an accounting for it in the day of judgment."

MATTHEW 12:36

The father of a boy with a bad temper gave his son a bag of nails, telling him to hammer a nail into the fence each time he was upset. The first day the boy drove 37 nails into the fence. Then it gradually dwindled down. He discovered it was easier to hold his temper than to drive those nails into the fence.

The day came when the boy didn't lose his temper at all. He told his father about it and the father suggested that the boy now pull out one nail for each day that he was able to hold his temper. The days passed and the young boy was finally able to tell his father that all the nails were gone. The father took his son by the hand and led him to the fence.

"You have done well, but look at the holes in the fence. When you say things in anger, they leave a scar. You can put a knife in a man and draw it out. It won't matter how many times you say 'I'm sorry,' the wound is still there."

Father, help us to think before we say careless or hurtful things. *Amen*

Loyalty and Love

Love is patient.
1 CORINTHIANS 13:4

Hudson Taylor had a great philosophy: "He must move men through God, by prayer."

Once in China and very alone, he asked God to send him a wife and God did. Maria served to steady Hudson's faith; she brought common sense and balance to the marriage and she insisted that he take holidays. Under the influence of her less mercurial, yet joyful temperament, he shed those moods of melancholy; he was able to discuss every matter with her while forgetting to be introspective.

Hudson became more assured; together they had such a reservoir of love that it splashed over to refresh all who came near them. She helped to improve his grammar; as a lady she "polished" him. The overriding factor in their marriage was an equal uninhibited loyalty to their vocation. Without Maria, Hudson might not have been able to make the impact in China that he did.

Father, may we commit to love and loyalty and to be united in our dedication to You. *Amen*

Willing Submission

*You wives, be submissive to your own husbands
so that even if any of them are disobedient
to the word, they may be won without
a word by the behavior of their wives.*

1 PETER 3:1

John C. Broger said, "Since the marriage relationship is to reflect the relationship between Jesus Christ and His Church, it is imperative that biblical submission and love be practiced in all of its aspects between husband and wife."

Elisabeth Elliot wrote, "Supreme authority in both church and home has been divinely vested in the male as the representative of Christ, who is Head of the church. It is in willing submission rather than grudging capitulation that the woman in the church (whether married or single) and the wife in the home find their fulfillment."

God, help us to fully understand Your words about submission and to willingly submit. *Amen*

September 9

Held in Honor

*Marriage should be honored by all,
and the marriage bed kept pure.*
HEBREWS 13:4 NIV

One does not surrender a life in an instant. That which is lifelong can only be surrendered in a lifetime. Nor is surrender to the will of God, per se, adequate to fullness of power of Christ.

Maturity is the accomplishment of years, and I can only surrender to the will of God as I know what that will is. Hence, the fullness of the Spirit is not instantaneous but progressive, as I attain fullness of the Word, which reveals the will.

~ Elisabeth Elliot

Lord, You have given us this beautiful thing called marriage. We pray that those living together in relationships that cannot honor You will be aware of truth, Your truth, about the marriage bed. Lord, may the sweet aroma of Christ fill the hearts of men and women committed to You in their marriages. Bless them with Your abundance and grace. *Amen*

The Fruit of the Spirit

Delight yourself in the Lord;
and He will give you the desires of your heart.

PSALM 37:4

You were called to freedom, brethren; only do not turn your freedom into an opportunity for the flesh, but through love serve one another. For the whole Law is fulfilled in one word, in the statement, "You shall love your neighbor as yourself." But if you bite and devour one another, take care that you are not consumed by one another ...

The fruit of the Spirit is love, joy, peace, patience, kindness, goodness, faithfulness, gentleness, self-control; against such things there is no law. Now those who belong to Christ Jesus have crucified the flesh with its passions and desires. If we live by the Spirit, let us also walk by the Spirit. Let us not become boastful, challenging one another, envying one another.

~ Galatians 5:13-15, 22-26

Lord, may we be to our spouse the same caring, loving, tender, compassionate, gracious, sweet person that we want them to be to us. *Amen*

Green-Eyed Monster

Trust in the LORD and do good.

PSALM 37:3

All spouses get jealous from time to time. The fact that we do does not make it right. It is wrong to judge another and wrong to set unrealistic rules for another. When rules disrupt and tear down, they cannot be from God. There is a balance and every couple has to come to a place where they know they can trust God in the life of their spouse.

A lack of trust in God and the work he has done in our spouses' hearts is never warranted. All the counseling in the world cannot help one overcome jealousy if repentance and a desire to love and trust the way God teaches us is not in place in a marriage or in any other relationship. The heart has its reasons of which reason knows nothing.

~ Blaise Pascal

Jesus, You are our Hope.
We need You to show us our
wickedness and to cleanse
us from it. *Amen*

September 12

Bible Knowledge

Intelligent people are always ready to learn.
Their ears are open for knowledge.
PROVERBS 18:15 NLT

The Bible tells us to be ready to give account ... to give an answer to those who ask. We are mistaken if we think that we can get along with slovenly and incomplete knowledge of the Bible.

No amount of spiritual experience, or even the Spirit's help and instruction will take the place of the study God requires us to put upon His Word.

~ Katherine Bushnell

God, keep our faces seeking You and learning of You through Your Holy Word. Thank You for the Bible. Thank You that the words are true. Between the pages lies the wealth of knowledge we need to be exactly what You want us to be so that our lives will bring blessing and honor and glory to You. *Amen*

A Proclamation

*"Go into all the world and preach
the Good News to everyone."*

MARK 16:15 NLT

The word "preach" conjures up images of Sunday morning pulpiteering or crusade-style evangelism, but the Greek word *kerusso* that is translated "preach" simply means "to proclaim a herald."

A herald in ancient times announced good news that a conquering general was returning from the battle with the spoils of war. Likewise, we've been called by God to proclaim that Christ has won the victory over sin and death and that salvation is available to all.

~ Danny Lehmann

Father, I pray that we would proclaim a herald to the lost world around us, that You offer forgiveness, grace and love to all who surrender to You. *Amen*

Treasures to Cherish and Love

See how great a love the Father has bestowed on us.

1 JOHN 3:1

Our spouses are treasures that we cherish and love: We should always want God's highest for them. The marriage relationship should be exciting, warm and tender all the time because it is a union of two who are now one, and one in Christ.

If your marriage has lost its romance and sweetness, remember that the same God who created marriage is the same God who is available right now to heal you where you are. He will not let you down. He wants His highest for you, and your spouse.

Tender and loving Lord, how blessed couples are to be able to come together in love that cannot be compared to anything on earth. This married love, which embraces the love You have for us, is uniquely ordained by You. Father, bless us as we do all we can, with Your help, to ensure that our marriages will last and that wilted flowers will be replaced with fresh blossoms. *Amen*

God's Love

He will love you and bless you and multiply you; He will also bless the fruit of your womb and the fruit of your land, your grain and your new wine and your oil, the increase of your cattle and the offspring of your flock, in the land of which He swore to your fathers to give you.

DEUTERONOMY 7:13 NKJV

The pure, mere love of God is that alone from which sinners are justly to expect that no sin will pass unpunished, but that His love will visit them with every calamity and distress that can help to break and purify the bestial heart of man and awaken in him true repentance and conversion to God.

It is love alone in the holy Deity that will allow no peace to the wicked, nor ever cease its judgments till every sinner is forced to confess that it is good for him that he has been in trouble, and thankfully own that not the wrath but the love of God has plucked out that right eye, cut off that right hand, which he ought to have done but would not do for himself and his own salvation.

~ William Law

Lord, You are all love. *Amen*

Face to Face
with Death

*For the wages of sin is death, but the free gift
of God is eternal life in Christ Jesus our Lord.*
ROMANS 6:23

Christianity has no more precious possession than the memory of Jesus during the week when He stood face to face with death. Unspeakably great as He always was, it may be reverently said that He was never so great as during those days of direst calamity.

All that was grandest and all that was most tender, the most human and the most divine aspects of His character, were brought out as they had never been before.

~ James Stalker

Your death, Christ Jesus, provided the only way to eternal life for all who believe. We are humbled as we think of the price You paid and the unspeakable suffering You so willingly endured for us. How can we thank You but to come to You as lost sinners to be saved by the atoning blood You shed for us. *Amen*

The Hour of Death

This is how God showed His love among us:
He sent His one and only Son into the
world that we might live through Him.
1 JOHN 4:9 NIV

He came to Jerusalem well aware that He was about to die. For a whole year the fact had been staring Him constantly in the face, and His time had come at last. He knew it was His Father's will and, when the hour arrived, He bent His steps with sublime fortitude to the fatal spot.

It was not, however, without a terrible conflict of feelings; the ebb and flow of the most diverse emotions anguish and ecstasy, the most prolonged and crushing depression, the most triumphant joy and the most majestic peace swayed hither and thither within Him like the moods of a vast ocean.

~ Kristina Howells

Lord, the anguish You experienced was for us.
Help us, I pray, to never lose sight of every detail
of what You went through so that we could be
certain we will be with You for all eternity. *Amen*

Her Crown

*He redeems me from death and crowns
me with love and tender mercies.*

PSALM 103:4 NLT

There is a crown laid up for mothers. Mothers are so many things. Most mothers, these days, work forty or more hours each week and they still complete the long lists of things to do every day. They are there for homework, ball games, skits, they manage to treat the kids from time to time and rarely say no when asked to pick up someone else's child. They go to church and often sing in the choir and teach.

I'm a mother and just writing this makes me wonder, how do mothers do it? God's grace has to be real and very available. Otherwise, there would not be a mother anywhere who could come close to meeting daily demands.

God, there are no words in any language to express how grateful we are for our mothers. There is one word that You so graciously gave us to show them how much we appreciate them ... LOVE. *Amen*

September 19

Beautiful Women

*Teach the older women to be reverent in
the way they live ... but to teach what is good.
Then they can urge the younger women to love
their husbands and children, to be self-controlled
and pure, to be busy at home, to be kind.*
TITUS 2:3-5 NIV

True modesty is the highest grace and adornment of womanhood. Modesty is the daughter of chastity; and wherever the heart is clean, true modesty is sure to reside. A most deplorable lack in our modern life is that of true modesty in both men and women. The first of all virtues is innocence; the next, modesty. If we banish modesty out of the world, she carries away with her half the virtue that is in it.

~ Nuttily Altar

God, my body belongs to You, and I pray that I would take care of it and keep it pure for You. *Amen*

September 20

The Local Church

*Since we have a great priest over the house of God,
let us draw near to God with a sincere heart and
with the full assurance that faith brings ...
And let us consider how we may spur one another
on toward love and good deeds, not giving up
meeting together, but encouraging one another.*
HEBREWS 10:20-21, 24-25 NIV

The sweetest and most sacred memories of life are those of home and church. The local church may not be all it ought to be. I greatly fear that it never will be so long as it has to be made up of imperfect human beings like you and me.

However, after you have said the worst you can say, it will still be true that it is God's greatest gift to a sinful world – Christ is the head. The church offers itself to the community. It wants to help everyone, from the little child to the aged and shut-in.

I think we can truly say it will always give more in return than you can ever do for it. The church's one foundation is Jesus Christ the Lord.

Jesus, thank You for our churches and help us to love Your church ... the body of Christ. *Amen*

He Holds the Key

*God will redeem my soul from the
power of Sheol, for He will receive me.*

PSALM 49:15

The living Christ holds the keys of death and Hades. In death He destroyed the devil and abolished death. There was a transference of power from the prince of darkness to the Lord of life; from those strong hands which had grasped the keys with such indomitable energy since the time of Adam's fall until they were wrenched from them by a stronger than he.

Smiting him to the ground, the Savior cried, "I will be thy plague, O death; thy destruction, O grave!" And from that moment the supreme control of death and the grave and the resurrection has been vested in the Son of man, who holds it as the arbiter of our destinies and the representative of our highest interest.

~ F. B. Meyer

Lord, because of Jesus' atoning blood, we can
bypass a living death in hell and spend
eternity in heaven with Christ. *Amen*

Doing Your Best

*Prove yourselves doers of the word, and
not merely hearers who delude themselves.*

JAMES 1:22

Almost as many different definitions have been given of a saint as of a genius; but there are some very common errors on the subject. A saint is not one of those emaciated, rather foolish-looking people sometimes represented in pictures. Neither are they always on their knees praying.

Rather, their whole life is a life of prayer, for they are always trying to do good. They are heroes of unselfishness; but their unselfishness is not shown by doing extraordinary acts of service, but by doing the ordinary weekday work of life in an unselfish spirit.

Emily Kimbrough said, "Remember, we all stumble, every one of us. That's why it's a comfort to go hand in hand."

Jesus, we want to do our best for You. Help us,
we pray, to lean not on our own understanding,
but to press in to Your heart and learn. *Amen*

September 23

Love Personified

Serve one another humbly in love.
GALATIANS 5:13 NIV

It has been said that a mother can be almost any size or any age, but she won't admit to anything over thirty. She has soft hands and smells good. She likes new dresses, music, a clean house, her children's kisses, an automatic washer, and Daddy. She does not like sick children, muddy feet, temper tantrums, loud noise or bad report cards.

She can read a thermometer and, like magic, can kiss a hurt away. She can bake good cakes and pies but likes to see her children eat vegetables. She can stuff a fat baby into a snowsuit in seconds and can kiss sad little faces and make them smile. She is underpaid, has long hours and gets very little rest. She is the guardian angel of the family, the queen, the tender hand of love.

A mother is the best friend anyone ever had. A mother is love.

Thank You, Lord, for mothers. *Amen*

A Celestial City

Thus says the LORD, "Heaven is my throne."
ISAIAH 66:1

For the Christian, heaven is where Jesus is. We do not need to speculate on what heaven will be like. It is enough to know that we will be for ever with Him. When we love anyone with our whole hearts, life begins when we are with that person; it is only in their company that we are really and truly alive. It is so with Christ.

In this world our contact with Him is shadowy, for we can only see through a glass darkly. It is spasmodic, for we are poor creatures and cannot live always on the heights. But the best definition of it is to say that heaven is that state where we will always be with Jesus, and where nothing will separate us from Him any more.

~ William Barclay

We look forward to being in heaven with You, God.
Thank You for preparing a place where we can
spend all eternity with You. *Amen*

September 25

Devotion to God

Be on guard for yourselves and for all the flock, among which the Holy Spirit has made you overseers.
ACTS 20:28

He works on us in all sorts of ways. But above all, He works on us through each other. Men are mirrors, or "carriers" of Christ to other men. Usually it is those who know Him that bring Him to others. That is why the Church, the whole body of Christians showing Him to one another, is so important. It is so easy to think that the Church has a lot of different objects — education, building, missions, holding services ...

The Church exists for no other purpose but to draw men into Christ, to make them little Christs. If they are not doing that, all the cathedrals, clergy, missions, sermons, even the Bible itself, are simply a waste of time. God became man for no other purpose. It is even doubtful, you know, whether the whole universe was created for any other reason.

~ C. S. Lewis

God, we desire to be devoted to You.
Help us to do this. *Amen*

The House of Prayer

"Even those I will bring to My holy mountain and make them joyful in My house of prayer."

ISAIAH 56:7

In 1887, R. W. Church spoke about the House of Prayer in a message he delivered: "Here, in His holy House of Prayer, we may come on our day of rest, and be safe, if we will, from any thoughts but those of the world to come. Here we gather together for no earthly business, but for a purpose of one sort only; and that purpose is the same for which saints and angels are met together in that innumerable company before the throne of God.

If there is a place on earth which, however faintly and dimly, shadows out the courts of God on high, surely it is where His people are met together, in all their weakness and ignorance and sin, in their poor and low estate, yet with humble and faithful hearts, in His House of Prayer.

Lord, help us to enter into Your
House of Prayer. *Amen*

Analogy

*The lovingkindness of the LORD is from
everlasting to everlasting on those who fear
Him, and His righteousness to children's children.*

PSALM 103:17

Y ou spend years trying to get them off the ground. You run with them until you are both breathless. They crash ... they hit the roof ... you patch, comfort, and assure them that someday they will fly.

Finally, they are airborne. They need more string, and you keep letting it out. They tug, and with each twist of the twine, there is sadness that goes with joy.

The kite becomes more distant, and you know it won't be long before that beautiful creature will snap the lifeline that binds you together and will soar as meant to soar ... free and alone. Only then do you know that you have done your job.

Father, help us to learn to parent the
way You do, by reading Your Word and by
listening to Your instructions. *Amen*

Eloquence of Example

"You will know them by their fruits."
MATTHEW 7:16

I watched a small man with thick calluses on both hands work fifteen and sixteen hours a day. I saw him once literally bleed from the bottoms of his feet, a man who came here uneducated, alone, unable to speak the language, who taught me all I needed to know about faith and hard work by the simple eloquence of his example.

~ Mario Cuomo

Father, Proverbs teaches us that "the ways of man are before the eyes of the Lord." We pray that we will be the example You would have us to be: a godly and eloquent example before the world. *Amen*

Becoming Overcomers

You need to persevere so that when you have done the will of God, you will receive what He has promised.

HEBREWS 10:36

Most Christians know suffering to some degree. Your suffering may not be as profound as someone else you know, but it could be a lot worse than what I have gone through in my life. No matter what level of suffering one is experiencing, it is painful to them and it is real. When we look at suffering the way Christ intended us to, we can rest, even though the suffering is still going on all around us. He is mighty and able to handle all our suffering and we can be overcomers. Helen Keller once said, "Although the world is full of suffering, it is also full of the overcoming of it."

Lord, help us, we pray, to allow You to work
through our suffering whatever Your will
is for us through the hardships. *Amen*

The Infallible Bible

The word of the LORD is upright, and all His work is done in faithfulness. By the word of the LORD the heavens were made, and by the breath of His mouth all their host.

PSALM 33:4, 6

There is no book like the Bible. It is a miracle of literature, a perennial spring of wisdom, a wonder book of surprises, a revelation of mystery, an infallible guide of conduct, and an unspeakable source of comfort.

Give no heed to people who discredit it, for they speak without knowledge. It is the Word of God in inspired speech of humanity.

God, we love You and want to honor You with our lives. We can only do that when we know You. Help us to read Your Word and with the intention of allowing You to draw us into it and to teach us from it. *Amen*

October

Seeking the Lord

The LORD is my strength and song.
EXODUS 15:2

A young woman, living in England with her Christian parents, wanted desperately to be saved. She did all she could to make salvation happen, but even after attending many religious services she knew she was not born-again. She happened upon a small chapel and went in, not expecting anything to happen. Sitting in the very back of the building she was surprised by the message she heard from a rather elderly minister.

As she listened she was startled by his sudden stop of words as he pointed directly to her and called out that, "You can be saved now! You don't need to do anything!" God's salvation came to her and she then knew the peace of Jesus. Later that night after she had returned to her home a new creature in Christ, one that did not even have to make a plea, Charlotte Elliott wrote the hymn *Just As I Am*.

We thank You, O Lamb of God,
for salvation. *Amen*

Knowledge, a Precious Jewel

The lips of knowledge are a precious jewel.
PROVERBS 20:15 NKJV

We all know people who think they know something about everything. Interestingly, they are generally those who have little to show for all their knowledge. God has given each of us knowledge, and if we ask for more He says He will give it liberally. Since God is all knowledge, what a great one to go to for that special gift.

It is obvious that God intends for us to learn from people, places, animals, things and circumstances. However, we are not to forget that He is the giver of knowledge and His resources never run dry.

Margaret Fuller said, "If you have knowledge, let others light their candles with it."

There is safety and protection
in the knowledge of God.
Thank You, Lord. *Amen*

October 3

Hold Fast to
Your Anchor

*I am confident of this very thing, that He
who began a good work in you will
perfect it until the day of Christ Jesus.*

PHILIPPIANS 1:6

President Abraham Lincoln was a devout man of God. He had a keen awareness of what progress was all about, which was evident from his words: "The best thing about the future is that it comes only one day at a time: You have to do your own growing no matter how tall your grandfather was: Things may come to those who wait.

But only the things left are by those who hustle: Hold fast to the Bible as the sheet anchor of your liberties; write its precepts on your hearts and practice them in your lives."

"To the influence of this Book we are indebted for the progress made, and to this we must look as our guide in the future."

~ Ulysses S. Grant

Father, thank You for blessing Your children
with such amazing gifts. *Amen*

Prepared for the Storm

The work of righteousness will be peace and the effect of righteousness, quietness and assurance forever.
ISAIAH 32:17 NKJV

When a farmer asked his young applicant for his qualifications, he said, "I can sleep when the wind blows." This puzzled the farmer, but he hired him. A few days later, the farmer and his wife were awakened in the night by a violent storm. They quickly began to check things out to see if all was secure. They found that the shutters of the farmhouse had been securely fastened. A good supply of logs had been set next to the fireplace. The young man slept soundly. The farmer and his wife found that the farm tools had been placed in the storage shed. The tractor had been moved into the garage. The farmer then understood the meaning of the young man's words – because the farmhand did his work loyally and faithfully when the skies were clear, he was prepared for the storm when it broke. He could sleep in peace.

Lord, help us to take the extra time to do what needs to be done. *Amen*

October 5

Humble Us

Before honor comes humility.

PROVERBS 15:33

A truly humble man is sensible of his natural distance from God; of his dependence on Him; of the insufficiency of his own power and wisdom; and that it is by God's power that he is upheld and provided for, and that he needs God's wisdom to lead and guide him, and His might to enable him to do what he ought to do for Him.

~ Jonathan Edwards

God, You exemplify humility.

Please make us humble people.

Help us to learn at Your feet. *Amen*

October 6

The Value of Money

The Lord will command the blessing on
you in your storehouses and in all to which you
set your hand, and He will bless you in the
land which the Lord your God is giving you.
DEUTERONOMY 28:8 NKJV

As payment for helping with the shopping, my sons were given all the S&H Green Stamps, but they had to accumulate them all year. When the time came to redeem the stamps, their minds were always made up, until they entered the warehouse lined with exciting items. They would change their minds a dozen times before finally deciding on one thing they would share. This helped them to understand the value of money. Each year I watched as they made smarter choices than the year before.

There is so much for us to learn in this life. God does not hand it all over to us at once, just like I would not have given my sons a pocket full of money to spend. There are levels of learning. Richard Bernard said, "A godly man prefers grace before goods, and wisdom before the world."

Lord, help us to appreciate the value of money and to never place possessions before people. *Amen*

A Rich Harvest

"Observe how the lilies of the field grow;
they do not toil nor do they spin."
MATTHEW 6:28

To grow in grace is opposed to all growth in self-dependence of self-effort, to all legality, in fact, of every kind. It is to put our growing, as well as everything else, into the hands of the Lord and leave it with Him. It is to be so satisfied with our Husbandman, and with His skill and wisdom, that not a question will cross our minds as to His mode of treatment or His plan of cultivation.

It is to grow as the lilies grow, or as the babies grow, without care and without anxiety; to grow by the power of an inward life-principle that cannot help but grow; to grow because we live, and therefore must grow; to grow because He who has planted us has planted a growing thing, and has made us on purpose to grow.

~ Hannah Whittal Smith

May the harvest be rich for
Your Kingdom, Lord. *Amen*

The Faith Barrier

Without faith it is impossible to please Him.
HEBREWS 11:6

We hear much today about the sound barrier. At one time it was considered impossible to fly faster than the speed of sound. Now scientific progress has made this possible, and man has at last "cracked" the sound barrier; he has advanced beyond that point which he thought he could not go. But there is another barrier which poses a problem for the believer, which I like to call the "faith barrier."

It takes a great deal of speed to crack the sound barrier, but to crack the faith barrier requires not excessive speed, but simply standing still. There is no work, no movement involved at all — just believing, or trusting the Lord, keep on trusting Him, and keep on waiting on Him. This is a wonderful technique provided experientially for every believer.

~ R. B. Thieme

May we be children who exercise
our faith in You, Lord. *Amen*

King of Kings

He who is the blessed and only Sovereign,
the King of kings and Lord of lords.
1 TIMOTHY 6:15

Where is your allegiance? There may be times when rushing to the call of a leader is exactly what we are supposed to do. After all, it was Christ who said we are to honor our leaders. There are, though, priorities that we need to have in place in our lives so we will know when to rush and when to stay and complete the work at hand.

Samuel Stennett said, "Majestic sweetness sits enthroned upon the Savior's brow; His head with radiant glories crowned, His lips with grace o'erflow. No mortal can with Him compare, among the sons of men; fairer is He than all the fair, that fill the heav'nly train."

Father, may we always know
to whom our allegiance belongs.
Thank You for the timeless truths we learn
from the great saints of old. *Amen*

Spoken Softly

Be kind one to another.
EPHESIANS 4:32

A mother wrote about a long, hard struggle to win a home and clothe and educate her daughters with which she had been blessed. "But," she said, a bit wistfully, "all has been easy because of the little words of praise which have come! No matter how hard I work making a dress, when my girls say, 'Mother, how truly wonderful!' I am more than repaid. No matter how hard the day has been in the kitchen, the yard gardening, when my husband or neighbors show their appreciation, I feel so blessed and grateful. A soft word! A little word of appreciation!

How fine it would be if we could but sprinkle them about each day. How many burdens, grievous to be borne, would be lifted from weary backs; how many care-lined faces would break into ripples of happiness; how many nerveless fingers would quicken and throb with a desire to do more!"

Lord, may we speak words
that lift others up. *Amen*

October 11

Time to Play

And the streets of the city will be filled
with boys and girls playing in its streets.
ZECHARIAH 8:5

What will my boys remember when they've grown old and gray?
The pants knees oft were full of holes? Or the trout we caught that day?
Just what will they remember most? Two little beds unmade?
Or the fun they had at hide-and-seek the days that Mother played?
What matter if my ironing waits while I smooth out their troubles?
Take time to kiss those briar-scratched hands, and start them blowing bubbles?
Will they remember mud tracked floors whey they've grown old and gray?
What care they if each room is dusted, if I'm too tired to play?

~ Phyllis C. Michael

Jesus, thank You for including play in Your great plan for us. God, we love You, and are so happy You made us so that we can have fun. *Amen*

Motherly Understanding

*Wisdom rests in the heart of
one who has understanding.*
PROVERBS 14:33

Have you ever seen mothers look at each other in church when children are at the podium or singing in a youth choir or taking part in a Christmas play? Mothers have a look they share, as if to say, "I'm supporting your child as if they were mine."

How about when a really sick child is brought into a doctor's office? All the other mothers grimace and ache for that child and mother whom they don't even know.

Leo Tolstoy wrote, "All, everything that I understand, I understand only because I love."

Jesus, how blessed we are to recognize the hearts of understanding You have given mothers. *Amen*

October 13

The Center of God's Grace

The LORD gives grace and glory; no good thing does He withhold from those who walk uprightly.

PSALM 84:11

Grace is more than mercy and love, it superadds to them. It denotes, not simply love, but the love of a sovereign, transcendently superior, one that may do what he will, that may wholly choose whether he will love or no.

There may be love between equals, and an inferior may love a superior; but love in a superior, and so superior as he may do what he will, in such a one love is called grace: and therefore grace is attributed to princes; they are said to be gracious to their subjects, whereas subjects cannot be gracious to princes. Now God, who is an infinite Sovereign, who might have chosen whether ever He would love us or no, for Him to love us, this is grace.

~ Thomas Godwin

Lord, what beauty there is in those who have learned how to live in the center of Your grace. *Amen*

October 14

New in Christ Jesus

For the death that He died, He died to sin once for all;
but the life that He lives, He lives to God.

ROMANS 6:10

The world was visited by the Son of God. He told of heavenly things. He revealed the mind of God on subjects hitherto unveiled. What He had heard in a celestial school – the University of God – what no scholar or philosopher of earth had even imagined – He testified, and some received His testimony and set to their seal, experimentally, that God is true.

And so it comes to pass that the Bible – because it is what it claims to be, God's Word, conveying God's thought – gives us absolutely new ideas of the way of salvation, of the sinless sin bearer, of the risen Lord of life; and announces the simple terms whereby He becomes to the believer, the sphere of a new life – his Justifier, Reconciler, Savior.

~ A. T. Pierson

We are so grateful to You, Lord, that all things are new in Christ Jesus. *Amen*

October 15

Special Occasions

"I will abundantly bless her provision."
PSALM 132:15 NKJV

She took paper bags and made hats so grand, she colored signs that invited all the guests in. She baked a cake when no eggs were in the house, she decorated and planned and kept the secret as quiet as a mouse.

She made the favors from old fabric she was saving; she wanted me to have the things my young heart was craving. She did it all on nothing more than love from deep within: she made a party to remember for me, and a dozen of my dear friends.

Lord, the gifts You have bestowed upon us through our mothers' sacrificial love and giving are forever embedded in our hearts. Thank You that You taught mothers how to make do in times of need and how to lead us to that place where all our needs can be met. *Amen*

October 16

Secret Sisters

Never tire of doing what is good.
2 THESSALONIANS 3:13 NIV

Many churches today have a season for "Secret Sisters" – when a name is drawn and you shower that person with prayer, notes of encouragement, gifts or flowers. While you are blessing your Secret Sister, the woman who drew your name is blessing you. It is a great way to learn about church members and a wonderful means of blessing. Anticipation is in the air when the women come together for a time of celebration and to learn who their Secret Sister is.

It is a precious blessing to know someone is praying for you every day and has you on their mind, blessing you. Having a secret sister to pray for and bless does not have to be part of an activity ... it can be done individually. Think of all the joy it would bring to someone you decide to pray for and bless regularly!

Lord, we are so grateful for new friends You
bring into our lives in a multitude of ways.
Please bless our friends with
Your love in abundance. *Amen*

Lifetime Friendships

*The pleasantness of a friend
springs from their heartfelt advice.*
PROVERBS 27:9

Bertha Kenningham wrote that "friends are like the sturdy oaks that rustle in the breeze when the summer suns are gone ... Like the boughs of spicy evergreens pressed against our lives to shelter from the wintry blast.

Friends are like the low blooming flowers that break at spring to light our path ... Like the perfumed roses dropping petals of happiness around our door. Friends are like green mosses clinging close to running brooks ... Like the flowing streams spreading their moisture along the fields and tasking no reward or pay. Friends are like the shady nooks giving sweet release at evening's hush and copper bronze to delight the eye. Friends are like the gentle whisperings of a love divine ... Forgiving and forgetting without a tinge of bla'e."

Thank You, Father, for friendships, and especially for those that have been dear to us for years. *Amen*

She Worships

Come, let us worship and bow down,
let us kneel before the LORD our Maker.

PSALM 95:6

George Atkins wrote the lyrics to *Holy Manna*, which were published in 1819. He included a verse about sisters and how they serve and worship just like men. Women need to have a personal and intimate relationship with God where they can worship and serve Him independent of family.

Some younger women feel left out of the worship because they are busy with children and the cares of the home. But women can worship Christ while changing diapers or baking bread. God desires our worship, so finding ways to include worship in our daily lives is essential. Allow Him to help you find times in your day so you can worship the Father.

Abba Father, it makes no difference what activities fill our day; help us to make room for times of worship. God, we love You and want to lift You up to the highest place every day. *Amen*

Gracious and Merciful

*"I will forgive their wickedness and
will remember their sins no more."*

HEBREWS 8:12 NIV

Mercy is extended by God to us because He has the power to forgive. He made a way for a full pardon of our sins when he died on Calvary Cross. When His mercy is extended He also says He forgets. How wonderful if we could make it a practice of not only forgiving, but forgetting the sins of our friends and loved ones. What a glorious place this would be if we knew how to give pardons with no strings attached.

"I have had a very unsavory past," admitted a woman to the authorities in San Francisco, "but for years I have gone straight." With tears in her eyes, she lamented, "How can people get away from their yesterdays if others shove their past into their today's? I've tried to let the dead past bury the dead. But the state wants to make my past my present." How differently does God deal with those who penitently seek His mercy and forgiveness? He is all merciful.

God, You are gracious and merciful.
Help us to learn of Your ways and begin
to extend that mercy to others. *Amen*

God Pours Out His Love

We know how dearly God loves us, because He has given us the Holy Spirit to fill our hearts with His love.
ROMANS 5:5 NLT

Frequently at the great Roman games, the emperors, in order to gratify the citizens of Rome, would cause sweet perfumes to be rained down upon them through the awning which covered the amphitheater. Behold the vases, the huge vessels of perfume! Yes, but there is naught here to delight you so long as the jars are sealed; but let the vases be opened, and the vessels be poured out, and let the drops of perfumed rain begin to descend, and everyone is refreshed and gratified thereby.

Such is the love of God. There is a richness and a fullness in it, but it is not perceived till the Spirit of God pours it out like the rain of fragrance over the heads and hearts of all the living children of God. See, then, the need of having the love of God shed abroad in the heart by the Holy Ghost!

~ Charles H. Spurgeon

Holy Ghost, fill my heart with God's unfailing love. *Amen*

October 21

A Joyful Heart

A joyful heart is good medicine.
PROVERBS 17:22

An elderly Scottish lady who is a sincere Christian told the following: "I have two daughters who take turns coming to clean my wee house. Jean comes, and leaves everything shining, but she makes me feel I'm an awful burden to her. But when Mary comes, no matter how dull the day or how low in spirit I'm feeling, she makes everything so cheery, and makes me feel she loves to be with me.

They are both Christian women ... but aye there's a great difference. Mary has what this poor world sadly needs, the Christian with the loving heart."

Lord God, help us to gain an insight into the lives of those around us, and to show Your love and joy to them. May we always be mindful that we reflect You to the world. *Amen*

Appeasing the Conscience

"Truly I tell you, whatever you did for one of the least of these brothers and sisters of Mine, you did for Me."

MATTHEW 25:40 NIV

An evangelist could not convince a lady that all the good things she did would not avail in God's sight. Being very wealthy, she gave a supper to some poor people, and also provided clothes for them.

An inspiration struck the evangelist and he said to her, "If one of the guests thanked you very much for the clothes, but said, I must make some small return and rolled up his old clothes in a parcel and asked you to accept them in return, would you be pleased?" At once she said, "No." Then it dawned on her how useless were all her efforts to make herself better, and she accepted the Lord as her Savior and King.

Jesus, help us to give without regret.
Please bring into our lives those that need
more than a pat on the back, those who have
needs we can help to meet. *Amen*

October 23

Real Joy

"For God so loved the world that He gave His only begotten Son, that whoever believes in Him should not perish but have everlasting life."

JOHN 3:16 NKJV

In a hospital ward, a lady missionary found an undersized and undeveloped little Irish boy, whose white, wizened face and emaciated form excited her deepest sympathy. His own soul's need was before him, and he was awakened to some sense of his lost condition. Brought up a Romanist, he thought and spoke of penance and confessional, of sacraments and church, yet never wholly leaving out Christ Jesus and His anointing work.

One morning the lady called upon him again, and found his face aglow with a newfound joy. Inquiring the reason, he replied with assurance born of faith in the revealed Word of God, "O Missis, I always knew that Jesus was necessary, but I never knew till yesterday that He was enough!"

~ H. A. Ironside

God, thank You for eternal life and for giving us real joy. *Amen*

When God Tugs

"Permit the children to come to Me;
do not hinder them."

MARK 10:14

A twelve-year-old boy became a Christian during a revival. The next week at school his friends questioned him about the experience. "Did you see a vision?" asked one friend. "Did you hear God speak?" asked another.

The youngster answered no to all these questions. "Well, how did you know you were saved?" they asked. The boy searched for an answer and finally said: "It's like when you catch a fish, you can't see the fish or hear the fish; you just feel him tugging on your line. I just felt God tugging on my heart."

Jesus, You do love little children and You
want them to know You at an early age.
I pray that children will be presented
with the gospel message so
they can know Jesus. *Amen*

Duck!

Wives, be subject to your own husbands,
as to the Lord. For the husband is the head of the wife,
as Christ is the head of the church.

EPHESIANS 5:22-23

Men are able to handle some things that women aren't good at. We are different, after all. Many times, I tried to do my husband's part when I should have allowed him to handle the thing. I learned that I could trust God in my husband and when he had to make difficult decisions, I could rest in that trust.

We used to laugh that if he was wrong and the arrows started flying our way, I would simply duck and let him take the pressure as well. He has been with the Lord for many years now, but I will never forget the times we were able to walk together in submission to what God had taught us.

Lord, thank You for godly husbands. *Amen*

October 26

Keeping Watch

The LORD will guard your going out and your coming in from this time forth and forever.
PSALM 121:8

The veil is drawn from before the seer's gaze, and he beholds the progress of war, pestilence, famine, as they decimate the populations of the world. These are scenes that make the heart turn sick.

We ask, has God forgotten the race for which His Son died? Is it after all the devil's world, given up to the wild passions of demons, effecting their full designs through men? Is there no hope or help but that the corporation that is in the world should pursue its course until it drops to pieces before the disintegrating forces of evil? Then the veil parts, and we see "God within the shadow, keeping watch upon His own."

~ F. B. Meyer

How blessed we are to know, Lord, that You are watching out for us. Thank You. *Amen*

Full of Grace

*To each one of us grace has been
given as Christ apportioned it.*
EPHESIANS 4:7 NIV

God brings those into our lives that are full of His grace and their lives spill over into ours. It behooves us to be around saints who build us up by their commitment to Christ and to thank God for them.

As rivers, the nearer they come to the ocean whither they tend, the more they increase their waters, and speed their streams; so will grace flow more fully and freely in its near approaches to the ocean of glory.

~ John Owen

Lord, You have placed all around us men
and women full of grace. What testimonies
they exhibit in their daily lives. Thank You for them.
Father, help us to be men and women who will
leave a legacy of grace, Your grace. *Amen*

Holy Reverence of God

*Since we receive a kingdom which cannot be shaken,
let us show gratitude, by which we may offer to God
an acceptable service with reverence and awe.*

HEBREWS 12:28

In order to the attaining of all useful knowledge this is most necessary, that we fear God; we are not qualified to profit by the instructions that are given us unless our minds be possessed with a holy reverence of God, and every thought within us be brought into obedience to Him ...

As all our knowledge must take rise from the fear of God, so it must tend to it as its perfection and center. Those know enough who know how to fear God, who are careful in every thing to please Him and fearful of offending Him in any thing; this is the Alpha and Omega of knowledge.

~ Matthew Henry

God, we humbly bow before You in reverence.
We praise You, Holy Lord. *Amen*

October 29

No Place for Cowards

In God I have put my trust; I shall not be afraid.

PSALM 56:4

The wicked is a coward, and is afraid of everything; of God, because He is his enemy; of Satan, because he is his tormentor; of God's creatures, because they, joining with their Maker, fight against him; of himself, because he bears about with him his own accuser and executioner.

The godly man contrarily is afraid of nothing; not of God, because he knows Him his best friend, and will not hurt him; not of Satan, because he cannot hurt him; not of afflictions, because he knows they come from a loving God, and end in his good; not of the creatures, since "the very stones in the field are in league with Him;" not of himself, since his conscience is at peace.

~ Joseph Hall

God, I pray that those who are crushed from the brutal attacks of one they love will know Your love for them today. *Amen*

October 30

Being Prepared

Create in me a pure heart, O God, and
renew a steadfast spirit within me.

PSALM 51:10 NIV

When the morning sun is bright, and the summer breezes gently blow from the shore, the little river boat is enticed from the harbor to start on her trip of pleasure on the clear, clam sea. All nature seems to enlist in her service. The fair wind fills her sails, the favorable tide rolls onward in her course, the parted sea makes way for her to glide swiftly and merrily on her happy voyage; but having thus been her servants, and carried her whither she would, these soon become her masters, and carry her whither she would not. The breeze that swelled her sails has become a storm, and rends them; the waves that quietly rippled from her pleasure now rise in fury, and dash over her for her destruction; and the vessel which rode in the morning as a queen upon the waters sinks before night comes on, the slave of those very winds and waves which had beguiled her to use them as her servants. So it is with sin.

~ Morse

Father, help us to be prepared.

The Name of Jesus

God elevated Him to the place of highest honor
and gave Him the name above all other names,
that at the name of Jesus every knee should bow.
PHILIPPIANS 2:9-10 NLT

Jesus' is a precious name to all believers because it always reminds us that He is the Savior. It was the name given to Him by God when He came into this world. It teaches us the purpose of His incarnation.

It is His human name reminding us that He who is God also became man. Peter made much of this name in the dealing of the crippled beggar, and declared that there is no other name sufficient for our salvation.

Solomon said, "Your name is ointment poured forth" (Songs 1:3). Lord, we pray that we would grieve each time we hear Your name taken in vain or called out in anything less than reverence. *Amen*

November

Light Brings Perspective

*Jesus spoke to them, saying, "I am the Light of
the world; he who follows Me shall not walk
in the darkness, but will have the Light of life."*

JOHN 8:12

An artist once drew a picture of a winter twilight –
the trees heavily laden with snow, and a dreary,
dark house, lonely and desolate in the midst of the
storm. It was a sad picture.

Then, with a quick stroke of yellow crayon, he put
a light in one window. The effect was magical. The
entire scene was transformed into a vision of comfort
and cheer. The birth of Christ was just such a light in
the dark world.

Father of light, You not only gave us light for
our physical eyes, but the light of hope for our
spiritual eyes. Thank You, Jesus, that Your light
source will shine forever for Christians. *Amen*

November 2

Let It Shine!

You are a chosen generation, a royal priesthood,
a holy nation, His own special people, that you
may proclaim the praises of Him who called
you out of darkness into His marvelous light.

1 PETER 2:9 NKJV

In ancient Rome, there was a temple dedicated to the heathen goddess Vesta. At its altar, virgins ministered as female priests, and their duty was to keep the sacred flame ever burning. If it went out through their neglect, they were severely punished. How carefully they watched it by day and by night!

Imitate, O Christian, their example. Keep the fire of Divine love burning on the altar of your heart. Suffer it not to grow dim; let it never go out in darkness.

~ J. I. Boswell

This little light of mine, I'm going to let it shine.
This little light of mine, I'm going to let it shine.
This little light of mine, I'm going to let it shine,
ev'ry day, ev'ry day, ev'ry day, ev'ry day,
gonna let my little light shine. *Amen*

It's OK to Say No

The work of righteousness will be peace, and the effect of righteousness, quietness and assurance forever.
ISAIAH 32:17 NKJV

Dr. J. Wilbur Chapman had what he called "my rule for Christian living": "The rule that governs my life is this; anything that dims my vision of Christ, or takes away my taste for Bible study, or cramps my prayer life, or makes Christian work difficult, is wrong for me, and I must, as a Christian, turn away from it."

Precious Father, sometimes we feel pressed on every side and sometimes we simply need to say no to what someone else wants us to do. Help us to have Your wisdom to know what activities will cause our Christian work to become difficult and to be strong enough to turn away. *Amen*

November 4

Beautiful in Season

They do not push one another;
every one marches in his own column.
Though they lunge between the weapons,
they are not cut down.
JOEL 2:8 NKJV

In their Christian graces no one virtue should usurp the sphere of another, or eat out the vitals of the rest for its own support. Affection must not smother honesty, courage must not elbow weakness out of the field, modesty must not jostle energy, and patience must not slaughter resolution.

So also with our duties, one must not interfere with another; public usefulness must not injure private piety; church work must not push family worship into a corner. It is ill to offer God one duty stained with the blood of another. Each thing is beautiful in its season, but not otherwise.

~ Charles H. Spurgeon

God, may we be aware of when and how
You want us to do something, and to be
always listening for Your voice. *Amen*

Discipline in Love

Now no chastening seems to be joyful for the present,
but painful; nevertheless, afterward it yields
the peaceable fruit of righteousness to
those who have been trained by it.

HEBREWS 12:11 NKJV

Discipline is not God's way of saying, "I'm through with you," or a mark of abandonment by Him. Rather, it is the loving act of God to bring us back.

C. S. Lewis said, "God whispers to us in our pleasure; He speaks to us in our work; He shouts at us in our pain." Every one of us knows that there have been times when we would not listen to God or pay any attention to what His Word was saying, until finally He used a severe discipline to get our attention.

Father, help us to understand why discipline is vital to our growth as Christians. Bless those children who are disciplined in ways that distort Your truth and love. Keep them protected, we pray. *Amen*

Pick Up the Sword

*Take the helmet of salvation and the sword
of the Spirit, which is the word of God.*

EPHESIANS 6:17 NIV

When men and women of high position express their love for God the Father and make it clear that they would not or could not be in that place without Christ, it humbles us. God has blessed America with several presidents who loved Him and who were not ashamed to let their relationship to Him be known.

When Edward VI was crowned king of England, three swords were placed before him as tokens of his power. Said the king: "Bring another sword – 'the sword of the Spirit, which is the Word of God!' I need this sword more than any other to overcome evil!"

Omnipotent Father, we would take up the
sword of the Lord today to ensure that we are
well prepared for every battle for You that comes
our way. Help us to know that Your plans include
things that appear mundane to us at times,
but Your plans are right and good. *Amen*

Making Friends

Do nothing out of selfish ambition or vain conceit.
Rather, in humility value others above yourselves.
PHILIPPIANS 2:3 NIV

A new homeowner's riding lawn mower had broken down, and he had been working fruitlessly for two hours trying to get it back together. Suddenly, one of his neighbors appeared with a handful of tools. "Can I give some help?" he asked.

In twenty minutes he had the mower functioning beautifully. "Thanks a million," the now-happy new-comer said. "And say, what do you make with such fine tools?" "Mostly friends," the neighbor smiled. "I'm available any time."

Father, help us to be aware of those around us and to be willing to give of ourselves and our things to meet others' needs. *Amen*

November 8

Creativity to be Remembered

He has made His wonderful works to be remembered;
the LORD is gracious and full of compassion.
PSALM 111:4 NKJV

Many people try to imitate Christ, but fail miserably because they do not know Him. If we love Him and His work, we will study Him and know His ways.

God has an open book filled with all we need to know about Him and how to spend eternity enjoying His creativity with Him. It takes a move on our part to open the Book and devour the written Word. Oh, to be like Him!

God, You are the one true Creator of everything.
Help us to love You and love Your talents
so much that we will reach deep into the
pages of Your Word and allow You to
teach us Your timeless truths. *Amen*

A Special Gift

I will praise You,
for I am fearfully and wonderfully made;
marvelous are Your works,
and that my soul knows very well.

PSALM 139:14 NKJV

My three-year-old granddaughter has been told since her birth that she is a special gift from God. Now when people question her about who she is, she tells them, in her broken language, what she has heard all her young life: "I'm a special dift from Dod."

At three, and almost grown, she goes on to tell people why she is so special. She almost never forgets to tell them that she is made like Jesus and that He died on the cross for her. Obviously, she does not have a full understanding of salvation and being like Christ, but her youth has not stopped her from learning what many adults don't grasp: that Christ made us in His image and that we are fearfully and wonderfully made. Praise God.

Thank You, Lord, for making us in Your image.
We know we are Your special gifts. *Amen*

November 10

The Season of Spring

O LORD, how manifold are Your works!
In wisdom You have made them all.
The earth is full of Your possessions.
PSALM 104:24 NKJV

Springtime is a season of hope and joy and cheer — there's beauty all around us to see and touch and hear ... So no matter how downhearted and discouraged we may be, new hope is born when we behold leaves budding on a tree. Or when we see a timid flower push through the frozen sod and open wide in glad surprise its petaled eyes to God ...

For this is just God saying "Lift up your eyes to Me," and the bleakness of your spirit, like the budding springtime tree, will lose its wintry darkness and your heavy heart will sing, "For God never sends the winter without the joy of spring."

~ Helen Steiner Rice

Thank You, God, for seasons. Spring lives up to its name. It springs forth life, hope, and beauty while reminding us of the Creator of it all. *Amen*

Honest and Honorable

The rod and reproof give wisdom, but a child who gets his own way brings shame to his mother. Correct your son, and he will give you comfort; He will also delight your soul.

PROVERBS 29:15, 17

Verse 16 goes on to say, "When the wicked increase, transgression increases; but the righteous will see their fall." It is vitally important that we learn early on what is acceptable behavior and what is not.

Everything we have belongs to the Lord, but we are not to gain increase by taking what has not been assigned to our care.

God, help each of us to know the importance of being honest and honorable. Thank You that we as adults can learn from children. Help us to hold our children accountable, thereby teaching them responsibility. *Amen*

November 12

No Time for Foolishness

Do not answer a fool according to his folly,
lest you also be like him.

PROVERBS 26:4 NKJV

Most of us are foolish about things in life. Foolish people simply don't stop and think before they end up in some type of despair or trouble.

It was W. W. Dawley who said, "We have been given choices in life that determine our direction. God holds us accountable for the mistakes we make. As Christians we should want to be responsible. God gave Moses a rod, David a sling, Samson the jawbone of a donkey, Shamgar an oxgoad, Esther the beauty of a person, Deborah the talent of poetry, Dorcas a needle, and Apollos an eloquent tongue ... and to each the ability to use his gift. In so doing, every one of them did most effective works of the Lord."

Lead us, O Lord God Jehovah, to walk uprightly and not in the way of fools. *Amen*

Today's Choices

O people, the LORD has told you what is good,
and this is what He requires of you: to do what is right,
to love mercy, and to walk humbly with your God.

MICAH 6:8 NLT

There are choices in this life – we can choose how our day will begin, and have tremendous input into the way it will end by the choices we make. We can start out by complaining about everything around us: what others have done and are doing to interrupt our plans, or we can decide to enjoy what we have and what God has for us today that will be like no other.

We choose either to abide in Christ by trusting Him with our life or doing things our way thereby saying that we know more than our Lord. Considering the messes we have made in the past when we choose the latter, it would behoove us to fall back into the arms of the Almighty and let His will be ours.

Help us, Father, to decide to
choose You this day. *Amen*

Last Supper

"Give us this day our daily bread."
MATTHEW 6:11

A man's wife told him they had just enough food in the house for one last meal. He said, "OK, let's eat!" His wife prepared the meal, and the family sat down to eat. Holding hands around the table, he thanked God for His goodness. As they were finishing their "last supper" the doorbell rang. A church member dropped by to say his wife was cleaning out the fridge and freezer before leaving on a lengthy trip and wondered if they would be kind enough to use up the items so they would not be wasted.

God provided an answer to a specific prayer and He provided through a couple who had no idea these people were eating their last meal. It was the work of the Holy Spirit through prayer that caused this miracle work of God.

You are our provision,
Father. Thank You. *Amen*

Fools Rush In

Many are the afflictions of the righteous;
but the LORD delivers him out of them all.

PSALM 34:19

We need to know when to get involved and when to stay out of the way. Many times when God is working in a person's life and we see them struggling and even hurting, we want to help. If God wants us to move in, He will tell us. He will tell us if we are walking with Him and our relationship is such that we can hear what He says.

Every person's hardship is not a signal for us to rush in. Some hurts are designed to help us to deal with issues in our lives. God so graciously leads us to help where He wants us to help and where our help can bring honor to Him.

Jesus, help us to refrain from trying to do the work of the Holy Spirit. Help us to be discerning instead of rushing in to help. *Amen*

November 16

Mothers Who Care

"Do not worry about tomorrow,
for tomorrow will worry about its own things."
MATTHEW 6:34 NKJV

Women do worry, but we prefer to say we care. Oh, how many times have we heard that Mother cared? Her caring was matched only by her love. She could not fall asleep until she knew all of her children were asleep and safe. She could not eat a meal until she knew they were fed. She was not able to completely relax during the day the school bus had arrived with her little ones.

Yes, she worried. Oops! I mean, she cared. She cared so much that those same cares have been passed down to the next generation.

Bless mothers who care, Lord. *Amen*

God, Our Rescuer

Defend the weak and the fatherless;
uphold the cause of the poor and the oppressed.
Rescue the weak and the needy.

PSALM 82:3-4 NIV

It is the needy whom God hears in prayer. To approach the throne of an eastern king with a petition, one must needs bear costly gifts to win his favor. But ours is a God of grace. "Like as a father pitieth his children, so the Lord pitieth them that fear Him."

He asks no gift of gold or gems. But bending down to us in infinite love He says, "My child, how needy are you? What heavy burden is upon you? What grievous sorrow is darkening your faith? What fear of future ill is shadowing your pathway? What spiritual thirst do you want slaked? What barrenness of soul enriched? How hungry, how helpless, how faint, how hopeless are you? What do you need this hour? For I will deliver the needy."

~ James McConkey

Father, may we come to You in prayer and
draw from You all we need. *Amen*

Delivering the Needy

He will deliver the needy when he cries for help,
the afflicted also, and him who has no helper.

PSALM 72:12

"For He shall deliver the needy ... and him that hath no helper." Do not be too afraid of getting into the spot where you have no helper, for that is the spot where, like Jacob, you will meet a delivering God.

Do not be too anxious to be free from needs, unless you want to be free from prayer power. Accept them just as God sends them or permits them. The moment you come to a need, remember also that you have come to a promise. "He shall deliver the needy." To miss a need may be to miss a miracle. As soon as one appears in your life, do not begin to worry because it is there, but praise God because it is to be supplied.

Praise You, God, for my needs
that You want to meet. *Amen*

Treasure Awaits

The word of God is living and active.
HEBREWS 4:12

A minister stressed the importance of reading Scripture each time as if it was the first, allowing God to speak through His word what He wants us to glean from its pages. Reading the Bible is like a new treasure hunt every day. Morsels that seemed unavailable before are now clearly there for the gathering. The Bible provides what we need to live in these times of uncertainty.

Many are grasping for the newest fad, only to find after a while that they have nothing substantial to rely on. Treasures await the one who takes the Word of God in hand and carefully moves from page to page seeking nuggets for life. Such moments each day can make a world of difference in a life that has no hope or direction.

Lord, thank You for blessing us with Your Word that is filled with treasures that never run out. *Amen*

Fit for Service

Stephen cried out with a loud voice,
"Lord, do not hold this sin against them!"
ACTS 7:60

Thousands of Christians have had to lay their lives down for the cause of Christ. Most of us today can't recall the last time, if there has ever been one, when we have had to take a stand for our beliefs. Should that occur, would you be found standing? Remember, it is most difficult to be counted in a crowd when you are sitting in the back row, or when you have not been ground and milled for His service.

"Corn, until it is pressed through the mill and is ground to powder, is not fit for bread. God so deals with us: He grinds us with grief and pain until we turn to dust, and then we are fit bread for His mansion."

~ Anne Bradstreet

God, may we be willing to stand for You,
even under persecution. *Amen*

The Highest Expression

I will be glad and rejoice in You;
I will sing the praises of Your name, O Most High.
PSALM 9:2 NIV

Worship is the highest expression of that for which we are created. In true worship, God is all that matters. True worship is spiritual – we are in the Spirit.

The Holy Spirit in us is to be the life of the glorified Jesus, as expressed in Psalm 66:1-4: "Shout joyfully to God, all the earth; sing the glory of His name; make His praise glorious. Say to God, 'How awesome are Your works! All the earth will worship You and will sing praises to You; they will sing praises to Your name.'"

God in heaven, we worship You,
we adore You, we honor You. *Amen*

Serving God

Serve the LORD with gladness.
PSALM 100:2

Has the way in which you have been serving God betrayed you into exhaustion? If so, then rally your affections. Where did you start the service from? From your own sympathy or from the basis of the Redemption of Jesus Christ?

Continually go back to the foundation of your affections and recollect where the source of power is. You have no right to say – "O Lord, I am so exhausted." He saved and sanctified you in order to exhaust you. Be exhausted for God, but remember that your supply comes from Him. "All my fresh springs shall be in Thee."

~ Oswald Chambers

We know that we need to be refreshed from Your supply, Lord, so we can serve without becoming exhausted. *Amen*

Our Heritage

For to me, to live is Christ and to die is gain.
PHILIPPIANS 1:21

Jesus had only three years to accomplish His life-work. If we remember how quickly three years in an ordinary life pass away, and how little at their close there usually is to show for them, we shall see what must have been the size and quality of that character, and what the unity and intensity of design in that life, which in so marvelously short a time made such a deep and ineffaceable impression on the world, and left to mankind such a heritage of truth and influence.

~ James Stalker

Thank You, Jesus, for our heritage
as Christians. Help us to pass this on
to the next generation. *Amen*

Preaching Heaven

... The kingdom of heaven is at hand.
MATTHEW 3:2

The commonest phrase of His (Jesus') preaching was "the kingdom of God." It will be remembered how many of His parables begin with "The kingdom of heaven is like" so and so. He said, "I must preach the kingdom of God to other cities also," thereby characterizing the matter of His preaching; and in the same way He is said to have sent forth the apostles "to preach the kingdom of God."

He did not invent the phrase. It was a historical one handed down from the past, and was common in the mouths of His contemporaries. The Baptist had made large use of it, the burden of his message being, "The kingdom of God is at hand."

~ James Stalker

Jesus, may we learn how to preach
the kingdom of God by listening
to what You preached. *Amen*

Getting Inspired

Commit your works to the LORD,
and your thoughts will be established.

PROVERBS 16:3 NKJV

Ernest Newman once said, "The great composer ... does not set to work because he is inspired, but becomes inspired because he is working. Beethoven, Wagner, Bach, and Mozart settled down day after day to the job in hand with as much regularity as an accountant settles down each day to his figures. They didn't waste time waiting for inspiration." It would appear that getting-a-move-on is the next step!

"Not only does inspiration from the Lord compensate for want of facts; it also induces men by self-discipline, to conform in their personal conduct and in their dealings one with another to the highest standards they know. In other words, it gives men the capacity which distinguishes wisdom from knowledge."

~ M. G. Romney

Jesus, we pray that we would be inspired
to do what You have called us to do
when we get busy trying. *Amen*

Wisdom about Success

*Now then, my children, listen to me [wisdom];
blessed are those who keep my ways. Listen to
my instruction and be wise; do not disregard it.
Blessed are those who listen to me, watching daily
at my doors, waiting at my doorway. For those who
find me find life and receive favor from the LORD.*
PROVERBS 8:32-35 NIV

King Solomon was favored by the Lord God because he listened and sought wisdom about all else to lead God's people. God blessed him with an abundance of wealth and so much more.

Looking at Solomon's life should ignite a burning desire in each of us to seek the Father's wisdom. How foolish it is to tackle the problems of the world today on our own or even with an army of those just like us. God is the source of all we need.

Help us, dear Father, to not be so foolish as to not listen to Your words of wisdom about success. I pray that all our desires will be according to Your will. *Amen*

November 27

Worldly Ambition

Live in harmony with one another.
Do not be proud, but be willing to associate
with people of low position. Do not be conceited.

Romans 12:16 NIV

George S. Bowes comments on the futility of all worldly ambitions which is not accompanied by dedication to God: "Alexander the Great was not satisfied, even when he had completely subdued the nations. He died at an early age in a state of debauchery. Hannibal, who filled three bushels with the gold rings taken from the knights he had slaughtered, committed suicide by swallowing poison. Few noted his passing, and he left this earth completely unmourned. Julius Caesar, 'dyeing his garments in the blood of one million of his foes,' conquered 800 cities, only to be stabbed by his best friends. Napoleon, after being the scourge of Europe, spent his last years in banishment. No wonder Solomon comments the way he does about the bleak future of all who strive to succeed without full devotion to God."

~ J. Mike Minnix

Help us, Lord, to have honorable ambitions for our lives and to live every day for You. *Amen*

November 28

Trusting God

I will put my trust in Him.
HEBREWS 2:13 NIV

God wants men who will render service to Him for the very love of Him, even though they never have reward. You remember Job's great word: "Though He slay me, yet will I trust Him." How often is that passage erroneously quoted, as though Job meant to say, "If He slay me, it will be all right; there is something beyond it, I shall not lose everything." That is not the true interpretation.

The word "slay" goes to the deepest fact of his being, and he intended to say, "Though He slay me" – not "Though He permit me to be slain by my enemies" – but, "Though I have no future, and never see Him or His throne, though He blot me out, yet I trust Him." That is magnificent trust, and goes far beyond the trust that hopes for reward."

~ G. Campbell Morgan

Trusting You, Lord God, is what we pray
we will do. Help us to do so. *Amen*

Heavenly Growth

He went in the strength of that
meat forty days and forty nights.

1 KINGS 19:8 NKJV

Some Christians are for living on Christ, but are not so anxious to live for Christ. Earth should be a preparation for heaven; and heaven is the place where saints feast most and work most. They sit down at the table of our Lord, and they serve Him day and night in His temple. They eat of heavenly food and render perfect service. Believer, in the strength you daily gain from Christ labor for Him. Some of us have yet to learn much concerning the design of our Lord in giving us His grace.

We are not to retain the precious grains of truth as the Egyptian mummy held the wheat for ages, without giving it an opportunity to grow: we must sow it and water it. Why does the Lord send down the rain upon the thirsty earth, and give the genial sunshine? Is it not that these may all help the fruits of the earth to yield food for man? Even so the Lord feeds and refreshes our souls that we may afterwards use our renewed strength in the promotion of His glory."

~ Charles H. Spurgeon

Father, help us to grow daily as
we learn from You. *Amen*

November 30

The Goal of Prayer

"Then you will call on Me and come and pray to Me,
and I will listen to you. You will seek Me and find
Me when you seek Me with all your heart."

JEREMIAH 29:12-13 NIV

The goal of prayer is the ear of God, a goal that can only be reached by patient and continued and continuous waiting upon Him, pouring out our heart to Him and permitting Him to speak to us. Only by so doing can we expect to know Him, and as we come to know Him better we shall spend more time in His presence and find that presence a constant and ever-increasing delight.

This means that the soul which has come into intimate contact with God in the silence of the prayer chamber is never out of conscious touch with the Father, that the heart is always going out to Him in loving communion, and that the moment the mind is released from the task upon which it is engaged it returns as naturally to God as the bird does its nest.

~ E. M. Bounds

Father, please help me to never lose sight
of why prayer is important. *Amen*

December

December 1

The Watchword

"... Yours is the kingdom of God."
LUKE 6:20

Every new idea that has ever burst upon the world has had a watchword. Always there has been some word of phrase in which the very genius of the thing has been concentrated and focused, some word or phrase to blazon on its banners when it went marching out into the world. The French Revolution had a watchword: "Liberty, Equality, Fraternity." The democratic idea had a watchword: "Government of the people, by the people, for the people." The Student Volunteer Missionary Union had a watchword: "The Evangelization of the World in this Generation." Every new idea that has stirred the hearts of men has created its own watchword, something to wave like a flag, to rally the ranks and win recruit. Now the greatest idea that has ever been born upon the earth is the Christian idea. And Christianity came with a watchword, magnificent and mighty and imperial; and the watchword was: "The kingdom of God."

~ James Stewart

Lord, help us to proclaim the kingdom
of God as our watchword. *Amen*

Learn, Learn and Learn Some More

Make me know Your ways,
O LORD; teach me Your paths.
PSALM 25:4

We have freedom in our country so long as we don't allow it to be taken away by those who may not know truth but who are willing to fight for their own agenda. We have been so blessed by God with every possible resource to learn as much as we can so that we can give an account for what is truth, justice and Christlike. What an awesome place to live and what a great God we serve.

Do you think we should study, learn from every resource, and be prepared to take a stand for truth? "Learn not only by a comet's rush but a rose's birth."

~ Robert Browning

Father, help us to want to learn. You have provided all we need to fill our minds with truth. We thank You, Lord, for making such powerful tools available to us. Help us to reach out and grab hold of them and use them for Your kingdom. *Amen*

December 3

Opportunity

He watches all my paths.
JOB 33:11

Many are still sitting around waiting for opportunity to knock when it has already passed to the next door. God has opportunities unlimited for the one who will come to Him and seek the perfect place to serve Him, whether on the home front or abroad, the list is endless.

To improve the golden moment of opportunity, and catch the good that is within our reach, is the great art of life. It seems to be the fate of man to seek all his consolations in futurity.

~ S. Johnson

God, may we be prepared to take up the position and do the work at hand. *Amen*

A Call to Prayer

*With all prayer and petition pray at all times in
the Spirit, and with this in view, be on the alert
with all perseverance and petition for all the saints,
and pray on my behalf, that utterance may be
given to me in the opening of my mouth, to make
known with boldness the mystery of the gospel.*

EPHESIANS 6:18-19

As natural as it is for each member of my body to
be ready every moment to do what is needful
for the welfare of the whole, even so, where the
Holy Spirit has entire possession, the consciousness
of union with Christ will ever be accomplished by
consciousness of the union and the joy and the love
of all members.

~ Andrew Murray

God, before we open our mouths to pray,
help us to bow our knees to allow You to teach us
how to pray and how to remain in unity with the
members of the body of Christ. *Amen*

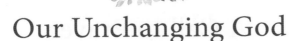

Our Unchanging God

*Jesus Christ is the same yesterday
and today and forever.*

HEBREWS 13:8

It has often been pointed out that the Old Testament gospel was comprehended in the phrase, "Do and live," while the New Testament gospel is comprehended in the reverse phrase, "Live and do." This is true in a very real sense.

We must remember, however, that it was the same unchanging God who said both. Unto us (of New Testament times) was the gospel preached, as well as unto them (of Old Testament times): but the word preached did not profit them, not being mixed with faith in them that heard it.

~ L. E. Maxwell

God, You are the one true absolute in
the world. How blessed we are to know
You and to enjoy that security. *Amen*

December 6

The King of
the Kingdom

*"Believe Me that I am in the Father and
the Father is in Me; otherwise believe
because of the works themselves."*

JOHN 14:11

The mark of what a kingdom is, is to be seen in the King. Christ now reigns as God and man on the throne of the Father. On earth there is no embodiment or external manifestation of the Kingdom; its power is seen in the lives of those in whom it rules.

It is only in the Church, the members of Christ, that the united Body can be seen and known. Christ lives and dwells and rules in their hearts. Our Lord Himself taught how close the relationship would be.

~ Andrew Murray

God, we pray that we would
be a mirror image of You,
the King of the kingdom. *Amen*

December 7

Heavenly Desires

I will very gladly spend and be spent for your souls; though the more abundantly I love you, the less I am loved.

2 CORINTHIANS 12:15 NKJV

The thing you long for summons you away from the self. Even the desire for the thing lives only if you abandon it. This is the ultimate law – the seed dies to live, the bread must be cast upon the waters, he that loses his soul will save it. But the life of the seed, the finding of the bread, the recovery of the soul, are as real as the preliminary sacrifice.

Hence it is truly said of heaven "in heaven there is no ownership. To him that overcometh I will give a white stone, and in the stone a new name written, which no man knoweth saving he that receiveth it."

~ C. S. Lewis

Lord God, help us to be willing to abandon everything in this world and be completely spent for You.

Amen

Time with Loved Ones

*Teach us to realize the brevity of life,
so that we may grow in wisdom.*
PSALM 90:12 NLT

A man worked so many hours that he had little time for his family and his five-year-old son missed his dad terribly. One day the father came home late after a long day at work and more tired than usual. His son so wanted to be with his dad, but the father begged his son to leave him alone.

Finally, the son asked his dad how much money he made in an hour and when the dad told him $20, his son wanted to borrow $20 from his dad. The dad asked why his son wanted the money and the son told him he was trying to come up with enough to purchase one hour of his dad's time. Time spent with those we love is a most precious gift from God.

Jesus, You are always available to us and we are so grateful for Your love and time. *Amen*

Fools for Christ's Sake

A person's own folly leads to their ruin.
PROVERBS 19:3 NIV

Mark Twain once said, "You cannot depend on your eyes when your imagination is out of focus," and that observation is so true. "A fool always loses his temper, but a wise man holds it back," says Proverbs 29:11.

We are all guilty of losing sight of what we are about as God's children, and we say and do foolish things. The foolish of the world "despise wisdom and instruction" (Prov. 1:7). And in Proverbs 26:3, we are told that, "a rod [is] for the back of fools." There is only one acceptable fool ... a fool for Christ!

Jesus, the pressures are so great today
for us to be like the world. God, help us to be
willing to stay away from the world's foolishness
and instead be fools for Christ. *Amen*

December 10

Smoke Signals

All glory to God, who is able, through His mighty power at work within us, to accomplish infinitely more than we might ask or think.

EPHESIANS 3:20

When the only survivor of a shipwreck washed up on an uninhabited island, he prayed for God to rescue him. He managed to build a hut out of driftwood to protect him from the elements and to store his few possessions. One day, after scavenging for food, he returned to find his little hut in flames, with the smoke rolling up to the sky and everything lost. He was stung with grief and anger.

"God, how could You do this to me!" he cried. Early the next day, however, a ship approached the island. It had come to rescue him. "How did you know I was here?" asked the man. "We saw your smoke signal," they replied.

Lord, You work in amazing ways to
show us that You are always watching out
for Your children. Thank You. *Amen*

Ordained and Sustained

Necessity is laid upon me; yes,
woe is me if I do not preach the gospel!
1 CORINTHIANS 9:16 NKJV

When we are called upon to undertake some work for God for which our strength seems utterly inadequate, then to believe that we may be strengthened with all might by the Spirit in the inner man, and to claim it, to act in the belief that God never calls to a work without becoming personally responsible for its accomplishing – this is the secret of spiritual efficiency and success.

F. B. Meyer said, "Be in me, O strong Son of God, to do by me all that Thou hast called me to; may I strive according to Thy working, working in me mightily."

Father, when You call us to a place of service, help us to move out, knowing that You are our efficiency and success. *Amen*

Treasures from God

As iron sharpens iron, so a friend sharpens a friend.
PROVERBS 27:17 NLT

I sat next to the bed of an old man, a friend for over twenty years, and held his hand. Hal was dying. We both knew these next few days would be his last.

Then he squeezed my hand, gazed intently into my eyes and whispered, just loud enough for me to hear, "Nothing is more important than relationships. Don't get overly caught up in your career, likewise, don't use people in order to achieve your goals, then throw them away.

No project, no program, no task should be pursued at the expense of friends and family. Remember, that in the end, only your relationships will truly matter. Tend them well."

Father God, as we consider the relationships we have as treasures from You, may we tend well to our relationships. Thank You for all our relationships and help us to serve You through them. *Amen*

December 13

Angels Unaware

Do not neglect to show hospitality to strangers, for by this some have entertained angels without knowing it.
HEBREWS 13:2

St. Peter instructs us, "Use hospitality one to another without grudging. As every man hath received the gift, even so minister the same one to another, as good stewards of the manifold grace of God."

~ 1 Peter 4:10 NKJV

In Acts 20:35 (NKJV), St. Luke tells us, "I have shown you in every way, by laboring like this, that you must support the weak. And remember the words of the Lord Jesus, that He said, 'It is more blessed to give than to receive.'"

Lord, may we be hospitable to those You send our way, willing to give freely from hearts of compassion, not expecting or wanting anything in return. Thank You, Lord, for teaching us the importance of opening our homes to our friends and the needy. *Amen*

Jesus Christ
of Nazareth

*We do see Him who was made for a little while lower
than the angels, namely, Jesus, because of the suffering
of death crowned with glory and honor, so that by the
grace of God He might taste death for everyone.*

HEBREWS 2:9

Of Jesus, Philip Schaff wrote, "Born in a manger, and crucified as a malefactor, He now controls the destinies of the civilized world, and rules a spiritual empire which embraces one-third of the inhabitants of the globe.

There never was in this world a life so unpretending, modest, and lowly in its outward form and condition, and yet producing such extraordinary effects upon all ages, nations, and classes of men."

Thank You, Lord Jesus, for all You are and for
coming to earth to save humankind. *Amen*

December 15

Astonishing Success

You will be prosperous and successful.
JOSHUA 1:8 NIV

Someone once wrote, "Jesus never traveled more than two hundred miles from the place where He was born. He never did one of the things that usually accompanies greatness. Yet all the armies that ever marched, and all the governments that ever sat, and all the kings that ever reigned, have not affected life upon this earth as powerfully as has that One Solitary Life."

"I have learned that success is to be measured not so much by the position that one has reached in life as by the obstacles which one has overcome while trying to succeed," said Booker T. Washington.

As we commit our ways to You, Lord,
please bless us and our labor. *Amen*

December 16

Pride Is Destructive

A man's pride will bring him low,
but a humble spirit will obtain honor.
PROVERBS 29:23

Pride is a terrible thing. It causes us to not accept things that God intends to be blessings in our lives and in the lives of those around us. In Psalm 119:21 we read, "You rebuke the arrogant, the cursed, who wander from Your commandments."

Father, we all need to learn that there is no room for pride in the life of a Christian. Precious Lord, forgive us for not accepting those things You have for us that will make us more like You. Help us to allow You to move in us and in the ones we love according to Your perfect plan, even when that plan doesn't look the way we think it should. *Amen*

Echoes of Life

"By your words you will be justified,
and by your words you will be condemned."

MATTHEW 12:37

Walking in the mountains with his father, a boy falls and begins to scream out in pain.

"Aaahhh!" The voice is repeated somewhere in the mountain: "Aaahhh!" He yells: "Who are you?" and receives the answer: "Who are you?" Angered at the response, he screams: "Coward!" The voice answers, "Coward!" He asks his father what was happening and the father says, "My son, pay attention." He screams to the mountain: "I admire you!" The voice replies: "I admire you!" Again the man shouts: "You are a champion!" The voice answers: "You are a champion!"

Then the father explains: "It's an echo, but really this is life. It gives you back everything you say or do. Our life is a reflection of our actions. This relationship applies to everything, in all aspects of life; life will give you back everything you have given to it."

Lord, let us give all we have to You so that we can receive all that You have to offer us. *Amen*

December 18

Personal Counselor

His name will be called Wonderful Counselor.
ISAIAH 9:6

Dietrich Bonhoeffer expressed his idea of the great Counselor in this way: "It is not experience of life but experience of the Cross that makes one a worthy hearer of confessions. The most experienced psychologist or observer of human nature knows infinitely less of the human heart than the simplest Christian who lives beneath the Cross of Jesus.

The greatest psychological insight, ability, and experience cannot grasp this one thing: what sin is. Worldly wisdom knows what distress and weakness and failure are, but it does not know the godlessness of men. And so it also does not know that man is destroyed only by his sin and can be healed only by forgiveness. Only the Christian knows this. In the presence of a psychiatrist, I can only be a sick man; in the presence of a Christian brother, I can dare to be a sinner."

Thank You, that You will never turn us away and that You are always available. We need You, Lord.

Amen

Desired by God

See how great a love the
Father has bestowed on us.

1 JOHN 3:1

A ndrew Murray wrote, "There is nothing on earth that awakens love and rouses it to activity so powerfully as the thought of being desired and loved. Let me endeavor to conceive how true it is that I am an object of desire to the Son of God. He looks out to see whether I am coming to Him or not. With the deepest interest, He would know whether I come hungering after Him, so that He may be able to bestow much of His blessing upon me. That would be such a joy to His love.

'Open thy mouth wide; I will fill it abundantly.' Thus does He stir me up to earnest longings. His desire is toward me. My soul, believe and ponder this wonderful thought, until you feel drawn with overmastering force to give yourself over to Jesus, for the satisfaction of His desire toward you: then shall you too be satisfied."

Thank You, Father, that You love
us and desire us. *Amen*

Toppled Walls

Yours, O LORD, is the greatness and the
power and the glory and the victory.
1 CHRONICLES 29:11

Unmovable walls. Just as the enormous walls of Jericho lay between Israel and conquest, so many impossible problems lay between us and conquest of what Christ desires for us. Unmovable walls moved. It couldn't happen, but it did. And it happened, not by "force or by might."

The Spirit of the Living God toppled the walls of Jericho, just as He topples the walls of sin in those who come to Him. Christ responded to faith, expressed in obedience, at Jericho, so He does today. He is our victory.

O Lord, thank You, for the victory
that is ours in You. *Amen*

A High Tower

Cast your burden on the LORD,
and He shall sustain you.
PSALM 55:22 NKJV

The carpenter I hired had just finished a rough first day on the job. A flat tire made him lose an hour of work, his electric saw quit, and his truck refused to start so I drove him home as he sat in silence. Walking toward his house door, he paused briefly at a small tree and touched it with both hands. Inside, he underwent a transformation. His face was wreathed in smiles and he hugged his children and kissed his wife. I asked him about what he did.

"Oh, that's my trouble tree," he replied. "I know I can't help having troubles on the job; one thing's for sure, troubles don't belong here. I hang them on the tree every night and pick them up in the morning. Thing is, when I come out in the morning to pick 'em up, there ain't nearly as many as I remember hanging up the night before."

You, Lord, are our high tower. Thank You that we can cast our burdens on You. *Amen*

December 22

Lord of the Harvest

Blessed be the Lord, who daily
loads us with benefits,
the God of our salvation!

PSALM 68:19 NKJV

Come, ye thankful people, come,
Raise the song of harvest home!
All is safely gathered in,
Ere the winter storms begin;
God, our Maker, doth provide
For our wants to be supplied;
Come to God's own temple, come;
Raise the song of harvest home!

~ Henry Alford

Lord of the harvest, thank You for everything
You give to us. You provide for us in ways that
are so amazing. We are grateful for the harvest,
and grateful, too, for the dry seasons for
they help us to trust You. *Amen*

The Most Worthwhile Word

The greatest of these is love.
1 CORINTHIANS 13:13

Anton was a Mongoloid. He could neither speak nor walk along. I did not know how much Anton understood really. Once I took his hand and touched his five fingers one after another and said, "Jesus loves Anton so much." The next week, immediately Anton saw me, he took my hand and with his fingers outspread he just looked at me with a face full of longing. "Jesus loves Anton so much," I repeated, touching a finger at every word. Then I taught him to do it himself. After that, every week, Anton showed me with his fingers how much Jesus loved him. The last time I saw him, I told him while he touched his left fingers with his right hand, "Jesus loves Anton so much. How thankful I am for that! You too, Anton?" "Yes," said Anton, as his face lit up. It was the only word I ever heard from Anton. It is the most worthwhile word that any person can speak to the Lord Jesus.

~ Corrie ten Boom

Thank You for Your Love, Lord. *Amen*

Human Hearts
Build Homes

Wisdom has built her house.
PROVERBS 9:1

Anyone can build an altar; it requires God to provide the flame. Anyone can build a house; we need the Lord for the creation of a home. A house is an agglomeration of brick and stones, with an assorted collection of manufactured goods; a home is the abiding place of ardent affection, of fervent hope, of genuine trust.

There is many a homeless man who lives in a richly furnished house. There is many a fifteen pound house in the crowed street which is an illumination and beautiful home. The sumptuously furnished house may only be an exquisitely sculptured tomb; the scantily furnished house may be the very hearthstone of the eternal God.

~ John H. Jowett

Help us, Lord, to know the difference between a house and a home and to make ours a welcoming home by allowing You to be the master builder. *Amen*

December 25

A True Friend

"I am the good shepherd; the good shepherd lays down His life for the sheep."
JOHN 10:11

Horror gripped the heart of the World War I soldier as he saw his lifelong friend fall in battle. Caught in a trench with continuous gunfire whizzing over his head, the soldier asked his lieutenant if he might go out into the "no man's land" between the trenches to bring his fallen comrade back. "You can go," said the lieutenant, "but I don't think it will be worth it. Your friend is probably dead and you may throw your own life away."

Miraculously he managed to reach his friend, and bring him back to their company's trench. As the two of them tumbled in together to the bottom of the trench, the officer checked the wounded soldier, "I told you it wouldn't be worth it. Your friend is dead, and you are mortally wounded." "It was worth it," said the solder, "when I got to him, he was still alive, and I had the satisfaction of hearing him say, 'Jim, I knew you'd come.'"

Jesus, help us to be willing to give up our lives for our friends, as You did for us. *Amen*

False Doctrines

Whoever believes in the Son has eternal life,
but whoever rejects the Son will not see life,
for God's wrath remains on them.

JOHN 3:36 NIV

False prophets also arose among the people, just as there will also be false teachers among you, who will secretly introduce destructive heresies, even denying the Master who bought them, bringing swift destruction upon themselves.

Many will follow their sensuality, and because of them the way of the truth will be maligned; and in their greed they will exploit you with false words; their judgment from long ago is not idle, and their destruction is not asleep.

~ 2 Peter 2:1-3

God, we need Your wisdom to be alert to the opinions in the world today that distort truth. *Amen*

December 27

Absolute Truth

*Listen to the statutes and the judgments
which I teach you to observe, that you may live,
and go in and possess the land which the LORD
God of your fathers is giving you. You shall not
add to the word which I command you, nor take
from it, that you may keep the commandments
of the LORD your God which I command you.*

DEUTERONOMY 4:1-2 NKJV

The Lord your God is one Lord." God is behind everything the final certain One. You cannot analyze, or divide, or explain Him, yet He is the one and only absolute certainty. He is One, all-comprehending, indivisible. When you have said that, you have said all. When you have omitted that, you have left every-thing out, and babbled only in chaotic confusion. If God is One, then the principles and the purposes of His government never vary. Dispensations and methods change; the will of God never changes, never varies, never progresses, in that sense.

~ G. Campbell Morgan, *Hallelujah*

Father, thank You for providing us with
a guide by which we can live meaningful
and fulfilling lives for You. *Amen*

Predestination

For whom He foreknew, He also predestined
to be conformed to the image of His Son, that
He might be the firstborn among many brethren.

ROMANS 8:29 NKJV

Corrie ten Boom wrote, "If you want to hear God's voice clearly and you are uncertain, then remain in His presence until He changes this uncertainty.

Often much can happen during this waiting for the Lord. Sometimes He changes pride into humility; doubt into faith and peace ... The Lord can and will do it."

Jesus, thank You, for intervening when we plan our lives outside Your will for us. Thank You that we can see times when You have saved us from certain destruction and even death. We love You, Lord, for working all things out for good. *Amen*

December 29

The Revealer

*Stand firm and you will see the
deliverance the LORD will bring you.*
EXODUS 14:13 NIV

It pays to wait on the Lord because He has revealed a way to wait on Him. He is the Revealer. Who hath directed the Spirit of the Lord (God the Holy Spirit), or being His counselor hath taught Him (see Isa. 40:13)? God the Holy Spirit is the teacher of the Word of God. And not only has He the power to do those things, such as solving our problems and meeting our needs, He has even revealed to us the way in which we latch on to this power.

It is through none other than the faith-rest technique, the moment-by-moment Sabbath, which is the means revealed by God the Holy Spirit whereby we claim this infinite power for every need in our life. So, we actually have, in effect, what He has provided the Holy Spirit, and the Holy Spirit reveals through the Word of God the way to wait on Him.

~ R. B. Thieme

Lord God, thank You for being our all.

Jesus Is Lord

That every tongue should confess that Jesus Christ is Lord, to the glory of God the Father.

PHILIPPIANS 2:11

When Paul wrote, "Whatsoever you do in word or deed, do all in the name of the Lord Jesus," he reminds us how in daily life everything is to bear the signature of the name of Jesus.

As we learn to do this, we will have the confidence to say to the Father that as we live in that name before men we come to Him with the full confidence our prayer in that name will be answered. The life in fellowship with men is to be one with the life in fellowship with God. When the name of Jesus rules all in our life, it will give power to our prayer, too.

~ Andrew Murray

Jesus, may we always bow before Your name in reverence of who You are and what You have done for us ... for all eternity. *Amen*

The Character of Christ

Who is like You among the gods, O LORD?
Who is like You, majestic in holiness,
awesome in praises, working wonders?
EXODUS 15:11

The life of Christ in history cannot cease. His influence waxes more and more; the dead nations are waiting till it reaches them, and it is the hope of the earnest spirits that are bringing in the new earth.

All discoveries of the modern world, every development of just ideas, of higher powers, of more exquisite feelings in mankind, are only new helps to interpret Him; and the lifting-up of life to the level of His idea and character is the program of the human race.

~ James Stalker

May glory, and honor, and praise be Yours,
our Lord, forever and ever. *Amen*